SAS: MY TRIAL BY FIRE

SAS: MY TRIAL BY FIRE

TRUE STORIES AND LIFE LESSONS
FROM SAS SELECTION

Des Powell

QUERCUS

First published in Great Britain in 2025 by Quercus

QUERCUS

Quercus Editions Limited
Carmelite House
50 Victoria Embankment
London EC4Y 0DZ

An Hachette UK company

The authorised representative in the EEA is Hachette Ireland,
8 Castlecourt Centre, Dublin 15, D15 XTP3, Ireland (email: info@hbgi.ie)

A CIP catalogue record for this book is available
from the British Library

All pictures are from the author's private collection and are
reproduced by kind permission of the author.

HB ISBN 978-1-52944-191-8
TPB ISBN 978-1-52944-192-5
EBOOK ISBN 978-1-52944-194-9

1

Typeset in Minion by CC Book Production

Printed and bound in Great Britain by Clays Ltd, Elcograf S.p.A.

Papers used by Quercus are from well-managed forests and other responsible sources.

For my mum and dad, Ellen and Leslie, who first gave me life, then gave me belief, but, perhaps most importantly, gave me the good old-fashioned common sense that I needed to sort this life out.

'Not everyone is capable of madness, and of those lucky enough to be capable, not many have the courage for it'
                                    – August Strindberg

'If it is endurable then endure it. Stop crying'
                                    – Marcus Aurelius

'And if you think tough men are dangerous, wait until you see what weak men are capable of'
                                    – Jordan B Peterson

CONTENTS

AUTHOR'S NOTE

For national security and confidentiality reasons, I've had to tweak a lot of details like names, places and dates in this book. Aside from the odd bit of research I've done online and in books, everything contained within these pages is based on my memory. Although I've done my best to recreate events as accurately as possible, it's very much my take on what happened.

Des Powell, 2025

A BOMB WHEN IT GOES OFF . . .

'I prefer peace, but if trouble must come, let it come in my time so that my children can live in peace'

– Thomas Paine

It was around the turn of the noughties and I was working 'The Circuit' – as in, private security, as part of a two-man team operating out of a coalition base in one of the major cities in the Middle East. It was hot, in all senses of the word.

At that time and in that place, you'd see a lot of mainly Yank and British troops on patrol, keeping the peace and guarding against insurgency. The British tended to keep a lower profile than the Americans. Partly for that reason, they were marginally more popular with locals. Or, should I say, 'marginally less unpopular'? Not quite as hated.

In our team, we kept an even lower profile. If you knew we were there, we weren't doing our job properly. My mate Neil and I would wear civvies, but if we had to leave our vehicle, we'd wrap our faces in a shemagh, the face-covering and head scarf that was enough to obscure what we called our 'white eyes' and maybe at first glance make us look like we belonged. It wasn't as though we expected to pass close inspection: locals would definitely take us for out-of-towners. But the point was that we looked unthreatening and it created an important point of difference between us and the Yanks, who often had a funny way of going about winning hearts and minds.

Beneath our shirts – despite the heat, long-sleeved to cover our tattoos – Neil and I wore chest webbing and carried our SIG Sauer sidearms. Our 'longs' – by which I mean our M4 assault rifles – were kept in the Toyota Land Cruiser, a deliberately scuffed-up 4x4 with plenty of room for the gear and enough punch to get us out of trouble. What we liked about the Land Cruiser was that you could use it as a weapon if needed. The four-wheel drive gave it power and the shell was tough. We'd be more than thankful for that before the day was over.

Setting out from the base each morning – and that morning was no different – our task at hand was orientation. It's an umbrella term that basically means being 'eyes and ears', putting the feelers out, getting the lie of the land and reporting back. We'd likely pinpoint whether a certain road was passable and, if not, what route to use instead. We'd identify no-go areas and places where local hostility was less intense. We were the ones filling in the gaps on the maps, the blokes to ask if you needed a steer on insurgency hotspots.

I don't recall exactly what our destination was on this occasion. As it happened, we never made it out of the city anyway. Not that day, at least. We'd found ourselves on a busy, narrow street with shops and stalls lining both sides and pedestrians crowding the pavement. It was a still day, with the sun-bleached canopies unruffled, the temperature at least 30 degrees and our Land Cruiser's air-con playing silly buggers as we sat in a line of dust-streaked vehicles and carts pulled by donkeys. Riding shotgun, I jiggered with the air-con, trying to coax it into life, at the same time keeping an eye on the traffic. I wore my shemagh around my neck. Neil wore a cap. Two peas in a pod we were. Wiry, sand-blown operators. Always alert. Always vigilant.

Gas canisters, I noticed. Many of the carts were laden with them. Power cuts were a fact of life in that part of the world. At night, the lights would go out and you could count to twenty before you'd hear the first generator roar into life. Then another and another, all over the city, all of them powered by cylindrical gas canisters. Locals would have them delivered the way we used to get milk at home.

'Hey up,' said Neil, driving and no doubt glad the Land Cruiser was an automatic. Best way to burn out your car's clutch? Take it for a spin around a city in the Middle East. He tilted his chin at the rearview and I swivelled in my seat. Swinging into view at our rear, announcing their presence with a mixture of noise, size and firepower, was a line of three American Humvees.

You've no doubt seen them in the movies. *Black Hawk Down* and that. Crewed by three or four grunts, the High Mobility Multipurpose Wheeled Vehicle, aka HMMWV or Humvee, always travelled in packs of two or three. If the idea was to establish a presence, then job done: they were formidable. Years back, they'd been lighter, but were vulnerable to IEDs ('improvised explosive devices'), so the newer versions were more heavily armoured. Each had a turret manned by a gum-chewing guy in shades (I'm sure there were Yanks out there who didn't chew gum or wear shades, but I never saw them) and the weapon would usually be a 7.62 calibre general-purpose machine gun, a pretty powerful weapon and ideal for what you might call day-to-day combat.

Two of the Humvees had the 7.62. The one upfront, though? That was equipped with a 50 cal.

The 50 cal is a big gun that looks scary and is expensive to fire. And because you don't always want to scare people and nobody wants unnecessary costs, it was rare to see one on a Humvee. Their advantage was power. A 50 cal is about taking down material rather than human targets and it can punch through armour, disable a vehicle and even go through an engine block. Here's a tip should you ever need to take cover behind a car during a firefight: crouch at the engine end where the block will stop most rounds. Most rounds. Just not a 50-cal round. Fire one of those into the front grill of a car and it'll go right through the engine and destroy the golf clubs in your boot on the way out of the other end.

In those days, we had a simple rule when it came to Americans in their Humvees: give them a wide berth. The reason was that they were trigger-happy trouble magnets and you were better off not being in the vicinity when it all kicked off. It wasn't just us who felt that way. The locals did too and, sure enough, the traffic in the street moved to accommodate the convoy as it made its way through. Everybody was of the same mind. We all wanted distance between us and the Humvees. As the convoy moved past – and the grunts didn't give us a single glance; we'd have worried if they had – and then slotted into the traffic ahead, waiting to make a left turn at the end of the street, Neil and I breathed a sigh of relief. There were five or six cars between us and them. Hopefully, that would be enough if anything happened.

And when the bomb went off, it was.

Just.

It was a car bomb operated by a lone suicide bomber. This guy would have packed his motor with explosives, probably strapped on a bomb vest, and then gone out hoping to locate a suitable target. Possibly he'd spied the line of Humvees earlier and tracked them, looking for his opportunity, waiting for the right time. I don't know. It doesn't matter anyway. What matters is what happened. And what happened was that, as the first Humvee rounded the corner to exit the street, the suicide bomber was able to draw up alongside the third one and detonate his cargo.

When a bomb goes off in the city, even up to three miles from your position, you know about it. You hear it. You feel the ground shake. Depending on your proximity, you might also feel a ripple in the air known as overpressure or a blast wave, the sudden release of energy caused by the detonation of the explosive. It's that hit of released energy that causes the most damage and the closer you are, the worse the devastation.

And if you can feel an explosion up to three miles distant, just imagine the effect when you're four or five cars away.

First, there was an almighty deafening bang, followed by a fireball as the explosives fired. The suicide car was blown apart, engine hurtling one way, wheels another, the guy inside disintegrated. The Humvee was crippled: tyres out on its rims, the grunt up-top a fatality, crew inside status unknown. Maybe in shock, maybe dead. I don't know.

5

And the blast wave. That deadly pulse as energy trapped and contained by buildings on both sides tried to escape and was funnelled down the street towards us. Pedestrians were blown away like straw in the wind, many killed or injured, horses and donkeys torn apart, canopies shredded, stalls reduced to kindling, all the windows shattering at the same time.

In the Land Cruiser, we were lucky. So bloody lucky. Ahead of us, cars were overturned or flipped onto their sides and the vehicle in front of us levitated and was turned almost at a right angle as it landed, but it shielded us. We did the up-and-down funfair ride but remained in position.

At the same time, we saw a dust cloud go up, before our windscreen went black with oil and there was a thump as something landed on the bonnet.

All of this happened in a split second. Everything from the first bang of the explosion to the thump as an airborne object found its way to our bonnet happened in the beat of a drum. The blink of an eye. That's how quickly and how arbitrarily death came to that street.

It was followed by silence. In the immediate aftermath, and for long moments after that, everybody who wasn't dead was in shock. I know from experience that, after a bomb like that in a crowded street, there would be between twenty and thirty fatalities, and another thirty to fifty injured. And the silence would soon be shattered by the screams.

But for the time being, nothing. Complete quiet. It was uncanny.

Neil and I recovered quicker than most and this we knew: the Yanks, having come under attack, would return fire. But with no target, that return of fire would be haphazard and erratic. No way did we want to be caught up in that.

The other thing we instinctively knew was that, in a combat situation, it's always better to do something than nothing. The advice they give kids at school to hide under a desk in the event of a school shooter? Not a fan. Most of those shooting deaths are from rounds fired at point-blank range. It makes better sense to put as much distance between yourself and the shooter as possible. You're reducing your chances of being hit. And even if you make the wrong decision, doing so can often lead you to the right one. Staying put is nothing. It's passivity and inaction. It's putting your fate in the hands of the gods, and we all know how capricious they can be.

So, do something. That's the watchword. And our first instinct was to get off the street and away from the crossfire, from which vantage point we might be able to do some good.

Correction: our first instinct was to clear the windscreen so we could see what the hell we were doing. Neil tried the wipers, but something was preventing them from working properly. I opened the door to peer out only to see that it wasn't just oil on the windscreen, it was blood too, and on the bonnet was part of a horse. I could tell it was horse. There was a mane. What was left of it.

Steeling myself, I stood on the door frame and yanked the horse off our bonnet. As I did so, I was able to get a good look up the street, the shock now starting to settle. The stricken Humvee was still there, of course – and no sign of any crew, which made me think the worst – while the middle one had also drawn to a halt. The leader had trundled on a way but was now in the process of turning back.

'Side street up ahead on the right,' I told Neil, who cleared the windscreen as best he could, creating a port hole through a delightful mixture of horse blood and engine oil. Peering out of our new window on the world, my eyes were drawn upwards and, for a moment, I thought they were deceiving me. Wedged into the walls of surrounding buildings, and looking like weird, oversized Christmas tree decorations, were gas canisters. They'd been flung far and wide by the explosion, probably from multiple carts, and they were everywhere. One of them not far away was coated in blood.

Now we were on the move and this was where the Land Cruiser came into its own. Neil shifted it into reverse and took it back, nudging the car behind then slamming it into a forward gear and shoving the car in front of us. The idea was to create enough space to mount the pavement and make a turn into the side street just ahead.

We bumped up onto the kerb and, scraping along the fronts of the bomb-scarred shops, made our way across the debris and over the pavement. I reached for my long and brought it to my lap. Also at my feet was a shoulder bag containing more mags that I slung across my shoulder.

Through the windscreen, I saw Yanks getting their act together now. The guys in the turrets were swinging their weapons around. No target, but even so they'd gone into payback mode. They were getting ready to rock'n'roll.

And then as we moved, I clocked something else, this time at street level: two guys who looked local, both wearing shemaghs. It was just a glimpse of them between stranded vehicles, but it was enough to tell me that they didn't fit in. They didn't look shocked. And they both had eyes on the Humvees.

We came into the side street. Neil grabbed his gear and we piled out of the Land Cruiser, M4s at our shoulders, crouched and moving back into the street to find cover. Now I saw a third guy clearly part of the same team. Again, he wasn't shocked, his attention focused solely on the Yanks.

The first Humvee was coming back, getting into position. That big old 50 was swinging around looking for a target, any target.

Be careful Des, I was thinking as we crouched. *You need to be sure. They could be civilians.*

And then I saw the AK47s and I was indeed sure. I indicated to Neil. 'Seen,' he said.

Things happened at once. Firstly, the guy with the AK opened up in the direction of the Humvees, emptying a mag at them. Why he did this, God only knows. It was wild, completely ineffectual and gave the Yanks something to aim at.

Next, the second guy turned out to have an AK as well. He'd spotted me and Neil. He brought his weapon to bear.

The middle Humvee opened up, responding to the mag fired their way. At the same time, I saw the third bad guy shouldering an RPG (rocket-propelled grenade), from which he fired a rocket. It fizzed off up the street to land somewhere near the second Humvee, but not close enough to do anything other than spook the Yanks further – which, of course, it did.

The second guy opened up on me and Neil, yet another wild burst that sent rounds pinging off the cars and buildings around us. He didn't get a chance to refine his aim. Crouched, I took the shooter, squeezed off, saw my rounds rake a car bonnet and adjusted during the burst. They call it 'creeping'. You aim low and track your rounds by sight, recalibrating your aim as you squeeze. I saw him go down. At the same time, Neil found his man and the second guy spun and fell.

Rounds from the second Humvee coursed along the street in search of the RPG guy who, with his two buddies on the deck, decided he'd had enough. The RPG was tossed away as he ran from the scene, presumably living to fight another day. The two wounded bad guys, meanwhile, were trying to follow suit. One was trying to help the other to his feet.

At which point, the first Humvee opened up. The Humvee with the 50 cal. He had the two guys in his sights and he wasn't about to miss. Couldn't miss.

He didn't. The two guys were vapourized. One second they were there, the next they were gone in a rattle of fearsome fire-power, reduced to scarlet vapour.

And that was it for me and Neil. No way were we about to hang around to try to convince the Yanks that we were on their side. They'd see guys with guns, one of whom wore a shemagh and . . .

Nah. No way. Fuck that. It was time to make like trees and that's exactly what we did. We clambered back into the Land Cruiser, got the hell out of Dodge and returned to base with a story to tell.

Added to which was a sense of having learned something. Every day's a school day, never more so than on an occasion when you engage the enemy. Even if you're not necessarily *learning* something as such, you're being reminded. Reminded of the need to be vigilant and try to read a situation. Reminded of the need for good teamwork and communication. Reminded of the need to take action rather than do nothing. Reminded of the need to anticipate trouble. As soon as Neil and I saw the Humvee, we went to Defcon 1 – because, like I say, those things are trouble-magnets.

And, of course, we were reminded of the need for training. If you're thinking, *Well, that's all very well, Des, but what does that have to do with SAS training?* The answer is this: don't be so bloody silly. It has everything to do with training.

In the situation I've just described, the average guy on civvy street would freeze. But being in the Regiment means doing the opposite of that, so that when things kick off is when you're at your best. You're not looking for the nearest desk to hide under. You're looking for an opening, an opportunity.

The potential to be that person is in us all. SAS training is all about locating that potential and bringing it out of you. You might say that applies to the Marines and Paras too and you'd be right. But a point of difference between the SAS and other regiments is that the others rely on numbers. In Para Reg, you might have 600 guys behind, you whereas in the SAS, you're working in a very small patrol and you won't have backup. You know that when you plan anything, you're doing it with the odds stacked against you. And from that comes a certain mindset. An SAS mindset. A way of thinking that involves taking responsibility, taking control, taking the initiative.

And – on a more practical, functional level – discipline. Cultivating a presence of mind that imposes calmness on a chaotic situation in order to come up with a plan. Also drills. Training is about drills. A drill, as I told somebody just the other day, is a routine that you perform over and over until it becomes instinctive, until you don't even have to think about it so that when bad things happen you know what to do. Getting shot at isn't nice and most people will panic. But the drill tells you: dash, down, crawl, observe, sights, fire. You don't just stand there. It's better to take action than do nothing at all.

And on that particular day, I knew what to do because training kicked in. Neil and I went into that mode and we carried it through. I'll go even further. Training is the reason that we won. A lack of training is the reason the bad guys lost.

And that's our job really – to make sure the bad guys lose.

CHAPTER 1

DEREK MEET ARMY

'Iron doesn't become steel until forged in heat'
                                                    – Anon

I'll say this for the British Army, they sort out your travel for you.

'Here y'go son,' he said, and that was it. At nineteen years old, I was handed my first Army rail pass. I've been using a version of it ever since, except that these days – after eight years in Para Reg, twenty in the SAS, and a long time on civvy street – it says 'veteran' on it.

I only need to look at that pass to remember the lad I was back then, green as the Wembley grass as I geared up for my introduction to Para training and what I instinctively knew would be a life-changing experience.

It was. And it's thanks to the Army that I've travelled the world and can speak a handful of languages. It's thanks to the Army that, when the time comes and the good Lord gathers me up, I can safely say that I did some good in the world and that my actions saved lives. And it's thanks to the Army that I haven't spent my life wondering what might have been. I've fulfilled my potential.

No doubt about it, it's given me a lot. And the first thing it gave me was that travel pass. Free rail travel. Wow, Derek Powell, you have arrived.

Before the Army, my direction of travel was a road to nowhere. I'd grown up in Sheffield, which in the early 1970s was a tough old place. You needed your wits about you, put it like that. I left school with smarts, but not much else. Certainly not a qualification to my name. Could barely read or write.

In Sheffield, all roads lead to the steelworks and, sure enough, I found myself there, joining the lads as we left the factory each night, wondering, *Is this it? Is my life already mapped out for me?* School, steelworks, marriage, kids – kids who would go to school, work at the steelworks, get married, have kids of their own, and so on.

As it happens, I bailed on the steelworks. My family circumstances changed when my mam opened a newsagent in Bournemouth. It was there that one day I caught sight of the Royal Marines in Poole Harbour. Although my exposure to the military had mainly been via war films on TV, seeing those guys in the flesh really put an idea in my mind. Already into martial arts and fitness by then, I saw myself jumping off boats and storming beachheads. Knowing no better, I decided that the Marines were the elite. That's what I wanted to be: a Marine commando.

The Powell family upped sticks again – this time to Milton Keynes for another newsies that Mam managed with my stepdad. It was close by, in Bletchley, that I found myself in an Armed Forces careers office making a dismal attempt at a Marines test.

My lack of education was painfully apparent. I flunked the test. One option was to wait six months, grow some brain cells and re-take it, but the Navy careers officer could see I had the bit between my teeth and so he directed me downstairs to where his colleague in Army careers was based. Down I went, feeling all at once deflated and hopeful. (Getting the bit between my teeth, determination, impatience . . . These are all characteristics I still have today, by the way, for good or for ill.)

If the Navy careers officer did right by me, then the Army guy was about to go one better. 'What would you like to do?' he asked, after I'd passed the equivalent Army test, apparently with flying colours.

'I want to do something special. I quite liked the sound of the commandos. Do you have them in the Army?'

He thought about that. 'I'll tell you what we do have. We have guys who are as good as them, called the Paras.'

'Paras, as in—'

'Parachute Regiment, son.'

I wasn't sure about the sound of that. In those days, I was scared of heights. Actually, I still am, even after literally hundreds of jumps. The difference is that I've learned to control and harness my fear.

But back then I heard the word 'parachuting' and imagined jumping out of an aeroplane. No, just no.

The careers officer looked like he'd heard it all before. 'It's a mode of transport, that's all it is. And the thing is, you do four months of basic training – that's fitness, weapons, fieldcraft, the whole business of being a soldier – before you get anywhere near an aircraft. By the time it gets to jumping, you'll be ready.'

He seemed pretty sure of himself, so I didn't bother arguing. 'And they're the best are they, the Paras?'

'There's one unit better. The SAS. But don't worry about them. You can't join the SAS unless you're in the military anyway.'

And that was it, more or less. I filled in some forms (as I was to discover, there's a fair amount of form-filling when you join the Army) and went home to tell my folks that I'd soon be out of their hair, first for an induction-cum-assessment – known these days as an 'insight course' – at Sutton Coldfield (more forms, a better medical, a bit of having to cough while somebody cupped my balls) and then on to Aldershot where my journey would begin in earnest.

It was May 1977. I'd signed my life away for nine years minimum.

Aldershot is a legendary place in Para Reg. Officially, the base is called Browning Barracks, but we called it Para Depot, or mainly just Depot.

And that was where I went, picked up from Aldershot station in the first of many Land Rovers that I would travel in during my Army career. This may not sound like much to you, but to me it was massive. That's when it hit me. This is me now. This is the future.

The next few days were to be a series of small but significant steps towards becoming a proper soldier. And if the Land Rover was the first, then seeing a Second World War Douglas C47 Dakota parked up on the barracks' approach road was most definitely the second. It stood there like a sentinel, a symbol of strength that only seemed to add to Depot's already forbidding reputation.

The feeling intensified as we drove onto the base. It was just what you'd expect. A vast sprawl of box-like buildings and concrete flats. I'd soon know it as home. I'd be intimately acquainted with the living blocks, the cookhouse, the classrooms, the marching square, the training area, the firing range and the assault course. But, at that moment, it looked like a collection of austere buildings, intimidating and confusing.

And busy. Recruits marching, some running, some forming up. I soon discovered that Depot was the base for a series of recruit companies at different stages of their training. Across the quadrangle, you might have a platoon nearing the end of their four-month stint, getting ready to move to Brize Norton for a month of parachute training; across from them another group preparing for the gruelling series of tests known as P Company; another, this one at an earlier stage of their training; and then mine, 439 Platoon, which right now seemed to consist of . . .

Me.

'Just me?'

'At the moment,' said the corporal, who looked a little unsure of himself. 'Tell you what, why don't we get you to your block and I'll find out what's going on.'

Climbing out of the Land Rover, the next thing to strike me was the shouting. In Army training, all communication takes place at top volume. Instructions are bellowed, orders are barked.

The corporal led me across the quad and to the area where the living quarters were located, not too far from the quadrangle where most of the marching and a good percentage of the bellowing took place.

You say barracks and people imagine what they've seen on

Full Metal Jacket. One big room, rows of beds either side and a space in the middle used by the sergeant major as he launched an assortment of imaginative insults on the hapless recruits.

The insults? Check. The rest of it? Not so much. Arranged over four storeys, each living block had a corridor down the middle and rooms either side, a series of little rabbit hutches, four beds to a hutch, separated by dividers.

In my hutch, I came across the first of my fellow recruits. He was lounging on a bed and looked up as I entered. We recognized each other right away. The two of us had been on the same assessment course in Sutton Coldfield, filling in forms, having our balls checked and running around to prove our fitness. I must have been told his real name, but everybody called him by his nickname: Scouse.

'That's because you're from Birmingham, is it?' I said.

'I'll do the jokes if you don't mind,' he drawled. From that moment on, me and Scouse were like that. He remained my pal during training and right through the Regiment. And that famous Liverpudlian wit came in handy on more than a few occasions.

The question remained, though: why were Scouse and I the only two recruits in an otherwise empty block? We'd been told that there'd be fifty or sixty other wannabe Paras joining us.

Scouse was none the wiser but less phased. Although the poor sod had already been there a day before I turned up, as ex-Territorial Army, he had a better grasp of the arcane and sometimes mysterious ways of the Army. 'Don't worry about it,' he said.

Sure enough, the corporal reappeared. Apparently, there'd

been some kind of mix-up and proper forming-up wasn't due to start yet. But since we were here . . .

'Private Powell, do you want to report to the QM?'

'The—?'

'QM. The Quartermaster, Private.'

Directed to yet another block in the warren, I noticed something as I made my way across the barracks. Although our living quarters went by the unexciting name of Recruit Company Block, others had place names. I'd soon learn that they were all battles for which the Regiment had been awarded battle honours: Bruneval, Arnhem, Rhine, Normandy.

Later on, I'd be introduced to the Regimental Charter, Monty's famous words, which started: 'What manner of men are these who wear the maroon-red beret?' It went on to list a great many attributes – toughness, fearlessness, duty, honour, tenacity and skill among them – and ended by saying, 'They are, in fact, men apart – every man an Emperor.'

Stirring stuff, especially to the nineteen-year-old Des. This was the legend of the Paras, the Red Devils, wearers of the maroon beret – aka 'the maroon machine'. I'd been at Depot less than an hour and it was already getting under my skin. Little did I know it, but it was going to be relentlessly drummed into me over the next six months.

At last, I found myself in the QM's lair, where I was provided with green Army trousers, or 'denims', black boots, a red PT vest and an old-fashioned helmet that probably dated back to the Second World War. Para helmets today are state-of-the-art and custom-fit. Back then? Not a chance. You counted yourself lucky if you didn't look like a complete plum. As for comfort, forget it.

The band that fit around my head was too tight, while the chin-strap was seemingly designed to prevent me opening my mouth.

Burdened down with my new gear, I returned from the stores to Recruit Company Block, where I shed my civvy clothes and dressed in the boots, denims, vest and helmet that would be my primary outfit for the foreseeable.

The corporal bundled us into the back of the Land Rover. It didn't matter that Scouse and I were the only new recruits at the barrack, he said. We would make the most of it, starting with a trip to the assault course.

I'd heard about the assault course. I knew it was famous for being the toughest in the British military, one of the hardest in the world. The kind of assault course that could break a recruit.

Ah, but it won't break me, I thought, as we bumped over a track that took us away from the barracks. (One of the few times I'd ever be driven there, by the way. During training we'd do the ten-minute journey at a run.)

We came to a wooded area. In there was the steeplechase, explained the corporal. 'And that,' he said, dropping the tailgate of the Land Rover and pointing somewhat unnecessarily, 'is the assault course.'

These days, you can go to an Instagram account called parachute_regiment_trg_company and see images of the assault course. Something that once had myth-like status in the imaginings of all recruits is now available to see in a couple of clicks. It's based at Catterick now, but otherwise has hardly changed in the almost-half-a-century since I first clapped eyes on it: a formidable, daunting structure seemingly constructed from tree trunks and reclaimed wood, with walls, tyres, rope swings, water jumps, cargo nets, the works – a structure whose job was to spew out an endless supply of exhausted, wet and dirty men.

Looking at it for the first time all those years ago, it didn't quite live up to the myth in my mind. *That doesn't look too bad,* I thought, and thought it for five reasons.

One: I was yet to give it a go. But when I did, I would not only eat those words but regurgitate them in violent fashion.

Two: I was a pretty fit kid.

Three: And a confident kid, too.

Four: I didn't know it then, but I already had the Para mindset.

Five: Because there was something else in that area, something that towered over the assault course.

This was the trainasium. And whereas the assault course looked hewn from the surrounding woodland, the trainasium was a Meccano edifice, hundreds of scaffolding poles bolted together with huge sticking-out lugs (and that was deliberate, by the way, just to make it more difficult to negotiate), arranged across various heights, the tallest standing at 60 foot. Some of the bars were wide apart and some narrow, added to which were ropes and nets.

The trainasium experience was what they called a 'bottle test'. One test involved having to walk – not crawl, not shuffle, but *walk* – tightrope-style along the bars, again at a height of 60 feet. You had to stand up on the shuffle bars, shout your name, rank and number, and then begin the walk across, lifting your feet over the lugs. Halfway across, you would stop, go down, touch your toes, say your name, rank and number, and then go back upright and complete your crossing – a total distance of about 12 feet.

Next, you climbed down to the level below, 30-feet high, for what they called The Lion's Leap. Standing with your feet together, you had to leap a gap to the platform around 10 feet below, then run along a narrow runway, jumping gaps and negotiating seesaw panels, before hurling yourself off the end and punching out to catch yourself in the cargo net.

Everybody wobbles when they do that. And, of course, there's the odd topple. Recruits fall from the trainasium, we were told, but that's the risk you take.

That was to come. The corporal, who saw us gawp, put our minds at rest. 'You won't be climbing that today. We just want you on the assault course, see what your fitness is like. Three times each. Ready?'

I gave it my all. On a count of 'Three, two, one, *go*', I was off like a greyhound out the traps, determined to make a good impression right away and keen that Scouse – who, although he'd never attempted this particular course before, had at least tried one during his Territorial Army days – wouldn't show me up.

It was hard. To look at, not so bad. *To actually do?* It's the water, the sludge, the mud. It's pulling yourself over a wooden structure, where your boots have at least some purchase, and then next meeting a brick wall, where there's nothing for your feet to grip. It's running, climbing, clambering, jumping, wading and crawling, while knowing that physically it's one of the toughest things you've ever done.

And then having to go round again. Not once, but twice. Then the corporal bundled us back into the Land Rover for the drive back to base. We'd done all right, he told us. There were some areas we'd need to work on and we'd need to train in our own time, but basically we were up to a certain standard. We had potential.

If we hadn't? If we'd failed at this first hurdle? Then we would have been told to go away and either do a lot of work on our fitness or think again about becoming Paras.

Meanwhile, I was beginning to feel a bit peculiar. It was partly something to do with the strap of my crash hat throttling me and partly to do with the three turns around the assault course. Talking to Scouse just before lunch, I suddenly felt distinctly nauseous, excused myself and went off to talk to God on the big white telephone.

It wouldn't be the last time. When basic training began, I was sick after the next three or four times I went over that assault course. I still think about it now. The assault course has that indelible association in my brain. I see it in my mind's eye, or even on that Instagram page, and I think about spewing.

THE TAKEAWAY

Throughout training, both in the Paras and then during Selection for the SAS, one of the biggest challenges – if not THE biggest – was the process of dealing with and overcoming fear. It's a subject we'll be returning to throughout this book time and time again because it applies to so many different situations in all walks of life.

Let's start with the trainasium. In the military, we have a saying: 'Fear stands for false expectation appearing real.' Never was it truer than when it came to that trainasium. In order to overcome my fear of that bit of kit, I had to remember, firstly, that the fear primarily existed in my own mind. Secondly, I had to go back to basics: I had to tell myself that I trusted in the system and also that millions of people had been there before me. If they could do it, so could I. I had the presence of mind to do that on my first go at the trainasium. Sickness aside, I made a fairly good fist of it, and I've abided by similar principles ever since, both in the army and in civvy life. Whether you're preparing for a parachute jump or gearing up to give an important speech, lots of people have been there before you, people who were just as scared as you are now. But they got through it. And if they can do it, then so can you.

CHAPTER 2

STAND BY. *GO*

'The triumph can't be had without the struggle'
– Wilma Rudolph

Basic training would involve what you might call an indoc-
trination into the world of Para Reg. All recruits became Para
historians, versed in how the Regiment's history can be traced
back to the early days of the Second World War when, in 1940,
following the fall of France, the British Army found itself in dire
need of strategies to counter the Axis powers. Churchill, ever
the visionary, recognized the potential of airborne forces and
ordered the formation of a parachute corps. Thus, the Regiment
began its journey with the establishment of the 1st Parachute
Battalion in 1941 under the auspices of the British Army Air
Corps.

The Para Reg baptism of fire came during Operation Biting
in February 1942. This raid on the Bruneval radar installation
in German-occupied France demonstrated the value of airborne
forces, showcasing an ability to strike deep behind enemy lines

and return with vital intelligence. The Paras had proven their mettle and there was no turning back.

As the war progressed, the Para Reg continued to distinguish itself. Operation Husky, the Allied invasion of Sicily in 1943, saw the Paras executing night-time jumps into enemy territory, paving the way for the ground forces that followed. Their tenacity and courage were again on full display during Operation Overlord – the D-Day landings of June 1944. Tasked with securing key bridges and disrupting enemy communications, Para Reg played a pivotal role in the success of the invasion.

It was during Operation Market Garden in September 1944 that the Regiment faced one of its most formidable challenges. Tasked with seizing and holding the Arnhem bridge in the Netherlands, the 1st Airborne Division, which included several battalions of the Parachute Regiment, encountered unexpectedly strong German defences. Despite being outnumbered and out-gunned, the Paras fought with unparalleled valour for nine days, embodying their ethos of never yielding. Although the operation ultimately failed, the courage and sacrifice of the Paras left an indelible mark on military history.

The Paras were involved in Malaya during the Emergency in the 1950s and in Northern Ireland, but the next major conflict was, of course, the Falklands War and the battles of Goose Green and Mount Longdon which . . .

Hadn't happened yet. The Falklands War was in 1982 and the young Des was going into basic training in 1977. Having completed Basic, I would join 1 Para, which didn't fight in the Falklands, staying behind on counterterrorism duty in this country, which is another story. Or not another story, as the case may be.

Anyway, back to Aldershot. After our brutal introduction to the world of the assault course, Scouse and I had been sent away and told to come back for forming-up proper. When I returned to Depot, I was to find that my fellow recruits had already begun to arrive. Forming-up would take place over a period of two or three days, with blokes arriving in dribs and drabs, and those of us who turned up on day one were kept busy, getting acquainted with the new ways of the Army.

For some, this was easier than others. Many had come via the Territorial Army; others had been junior recruits and, for them, army life was already second nature. I was lucky; my mam had showed me how to cook and do basic household chores, and I found myself called upon to help younger lads who hardly knew how to tie their own shoelaces, let alone iron a shirt or make a bed.

At the same time, there were those of us looking across at other platoons in later stages of their training – 438 and 437 Platoon were the two immediately ahead – and thinking we'd never be as drilled and disciplined as they were. They had their own blocks and their own instructors, and though they weren't yet qualified Paras, they looked the part: fit, assured and smartly turned-out. They barely glanced in our direction.

Next order of business: haircuts. Those of us from civvy street needed a proper shearing and, this being the 1970s, long hair was very much all the rage. With a few strokes of the clippers, off it came until we all had the regulation buzzcut. It's short because you don't want to worry about washing your hair in the field, and you don't want bugs in it. It's the same with beards. They get dirty. They need upkeep. I know I'm not the only recruit who, from that day to this, has kept the same haircut. It does that to you, the army. From your first day in Basic, you're picking up habits that become a way of life.

Next up, more trips to the quartermaster, the QM, where I was equipped with the plimsolls that we used to call road slappers. No insole, no padding, no arch support. Basic training equals basic plimsolls. Among other things, I also came away with green Army underwear and vests. I never wore either of those particular garments. One look was enough to bring me out in a skin rash. I kept them though. For almost thirty years, I stored those Army-issue pants and vests and never once wore them.

After a day or so, we had a full complement. There were sixty of us – sixty 'Toms' as we were called, a shortening of 'Tommy' that's since fallen out of favour and been replaced by the Americanism 'Joes'. Forming up for the first time in three rows outside Recruit Company Block, our training was to begin in earnest.

And it began as it would continue. With bellowing.

'Listen in.'

All orders delivered to the group began with 'listen in'. You heard those words, you listened in.

'Put your red PT vest on, your blue shorts, your green socks and black plimsolls. That is your PT dress. That is what you always form up in when you're doing PT in the gym. What are you waiting for? Fucking Christmas? Go. Fucking go, go.'

Colliding into one another like confused nine pins, we rushed to obey and then formed up in three shivering rows where the instructors cast a disdainful eye over us. The haircuts passed muster, but there were a few beer bellies (pointed out at top volume) and a lot of slouching (corrected again at top volume).

Somebody tried to ask a question. One of the civvy blokes, no doubt, because from the corner of my eye, I saw Scouse wince.

'When you talk to us, you stand with your feet together, do you understand?' came the response, loud and with added expletives. We called this corporal Throb because of a vein that stood out on his forehead when he was shouting. And he was always shouting. 'You stand to attention, have you got that?'

'Yes, sir.'

'Do I look like a knight of the realm to you? You will address me as Staff.'

'Yes, Staff.'

'Stand to attention when you address me as Staff.'

'Yes, Staff.'

And the kid never got to ask whatever his question was because the next thing we knew, we were ordered to sprint to the gym. 'When I say go, I want you inside the gymnasium and form up in three ranks. Go.'

Another command that would soon become very familiar. *Go.*

There to greet us was a muscular corporal in a PT vest whose speciality was the gym.

'Do you know what a beasting is?' he bawled at us.

Confused mumbles came in response. A bee sting?

'I said, do you know what a beasting is?'

'No, Staff.'

'Right. This is a beasting.'

We readied ourselves.

'When I say go, you touch that wall, then that wall and that wall behind me, and then form up in three ranks. Stand by. *Go.*'

We did as we were told, as fast as our little legs could carry us.

Black plimsolls slapped and squeaked on the polished wood floor as we dashed from wall to wall.

'Not quick enough. When I say go, do it again. Stand by. Ready. *Go.*'

And now everybody was really going for it, guys banging into each other, absolute chaos.

Touched the walls, formed up again. Our shoulders heaved as we tried to catch our breath. Sweating cobs, our faces were red.

'Right, that wasn't quick enough. Guess what? We're going to do it again. Go.'

Now the lot of us were going like Joe Stink, all coming to the same conclusion at the same time: that when told to do something, you do it as fast as possible and to the best of your ability – or you'll just have to do it again.

Without letting us catch our breath, he had us forming into lines and piggybacking to the wall, back again, then changing positions and doing it a second time.

'Right, now get on the floor. Twenty press-ups each. *Go.*'

It went on like that until, after forty minutes of running, sit-ups, piggybacks, dips, press-ups, pull-ups and rope-climbing, we were instructed to go back outside – double-time, of course – and form three ranks.

'Listen up. You have five minutes to change into your work dress. *Go.*'

Work dress was green denims, boots, green shirt and green recruit cap. Getting in and out of the correct outfits was soon to become second nature to us. Keeping it clean and ready to wear would be a priority and, therefore, a daily chore. Very soon the washing machines in our block would be running all hours of day and night as panicky recruits rushed to get their gear clean.

For now, we were just grateful to get the shit on quick enough that the instructors didn't bollock us. And we double-timed it to a classroom block where, at last, we were able to sit.

Now we were given a rough structure of how the next four months' training would unfold, how our CIC, or Combined Infantry Course, would boil down into two main components: soldiering and endurance.

For soldiering, we'd have lessons in fieldcraft, tactics, weapons, drill, discipline and so on. Endurance, meanwhile, was a case of getting fit and hard and meant lots of running, sometimes with full packs (known as tabbing, which we'll come to), plenty of marching and lots of time on the assault course and train-asium. In three months' time, we'd be tackling the dreaded 'P Company', the 'pre-parachute selection test' known and feared throughout the Army. If you wanted to be a paratrooper, you had to pass P Company. From that moment on, it loomed on the horizon. A day of reckoning.

We broke for lunch, which was in the cookhouse, a focal point of the barracks. The cookhouse was where we would take most of our food. Let me tell you, we lived for those meals. One of the first things we were told was to make sure to eat as much as possible. Para recruits were given more rations than the rest of the British Army (the 'crap hats' as we called them) simply because we needed the calories. Even with extra grub, we'd still be famished. And all of us lost weight.

After lunch, we double-timed it to another classroom. Back to school.

At first, the lessons were the total basics, the sort of stuff that half the company already knew anyway: ironing instructions, walking over to the cookhouse in twos (always with your 'digging irons', which is your knife, fork and spoon), how to lay out your locker, how to clean and 'bull' (aka 'polish') your boots, how to brace up and salute in the presence of an officer. The protocols of the camp. A crash course in the ways of the military. An introduction to discipline.

This was where our motto 'bullshit baffles brains' came in. Now I've heard a few definitions of this phrase, but as far as I'm concerned, it meant being ultra-disciplined in order to instil fear in the enemy. The idea was that you would meet your enemy on the battlefield and they would be dazzled by the discipline you showed.

After that came a run to the assault course for three gruelling go-rounds on it, followed by dinner and then double-time back to the block for block jobs: cleaning the bathroom and the showers, for example, polishing the floors, shining the windows, making sure all the lockers were neat.

By the end of that first day, we were all destroyed. Get used to it was what Staff told us. That was just your first day. And it was an easy one.

THE TAKEAWAY

From the outside, the military way of life can seem strange. It may even look complicated. It isn't. It's a simple, common-sense, pragmatic approach to the business of being. And the reason that so many blokes like me continue to live a focused, disciplined life, years after leaving, is because it works for us.

It's a principle that involves taking everything back to basics. KISS – 'keep it simple, stupid' – is the motto. A good soldier will always do the basics well, because when things get noisy or scary, that's where you'll go: back to basics. You can imagine how this translates into everyday life. Is your intention to spend the day in front of a computer? Get up in plenty of time to make your bed, eat a good breakfast, do some physical exercise and tidy your desk before you begin work. Do whatever else you need to do to get body and mind ready for a day at work.

Do the basics, do them well, and the rest will follow.

CHAPTER 3

BACK TO SCHOOL

'I have never let my schooling interfere with my education'
— Mark Twain

Our instructors were your classic 'hard but fair' types who, between them, had years of experience in training and in the field – Northern Ireland, Cyprus, Hong Kong, the Middle East. If there was conflict, they'd been there. We had three corporals. There was Throb; another one we called Boil, which might have been something to do with his Christian name, Lance; and Corporal Smith, who never got a nickname. (Corporal Smith was the guy who picked me up from Aldershot station on my first day and who, along with Boil, would later go on SAS selection and pass). There was also a sergeant and a lieutenant.

Most of the contact we had was with Throb, Boil and Cpl Smith, but it was one-way. You didn't get friendly with them. You didn't have a laugh or a chinwag. For now, their job was that of particularly brutal shepherds, getting us from one place to another and punishing us if we took our time doing so. Occasionally, the corporals would run a course for themselves, but mainly they put us into the care of specialists for detailed soldiering instruction. If the specialists were the scalpel, then the corporals were the hammer and chisel. Their job was to instil in us the fitness, discipline and toughness that had to be earned, not learned, and it was they who oversaw the daily routine, writing it on a board in the billet each night.

The routine could – and would, and did – change at a moment's notice, but it normally began with a 5.30 a.m. rise, then breakfast. There'd be some kind of fitness after breakfast – a beasting, maybe, or a sprint. After that came block jobs: cleaning the bathroom, cleaning the toilet, the sink, the showers. Floors would need to be 'bumped' – first treated with liquid polish and then buffed to a high shine. Lockers would have to be laid out properly with the doors open, boots in one section, shirts in another, socks in another, and so on. Beds would have to be pulled down, with blankets and sheets folded up like a block.

At around 8 a.m., we'd have to stand by our beds as a sergeant or corporal inspected the toilets, floors and corridor. He'd make sure bins were empty, beds were pulled back, bed block set out correctly, all of that. If there was something wrong – anything – there'd be trouble. I saw it more than once where a corporal came in, picked up a mattress and threw it out of a window, which is never a good start to your day.

With block jobs over, it was time to change into our working dress of boots, denims, green shirt, belt and recruit cap, grab any necessary notebooks or reference books and hurry to the first lesson, by which time it should be around 8.30 a.m.

The lessons in these early days were forty-minute chunks of

basic soldiering. They included camouflage, concealment and cover (as well as camouflage penetration), land and water navigation, obstacle crossing, good terrain use (i.e. selecting good firing positions but also good camping sites, observation posts), survival, evasion and escape techniques, map reading, weapons training, learning how to use a radio . . .

In other words, basic field skills, the art and craft of being a soldier. Initially, these were theory-based and taught in classrooms; later, we'd put the theory into practice on the ranges and training areas of Aldershot and further afield on the Brecon Beacons. For weapons, we'd be using the SLR, aka the L1A1 Self-Loading Rifle, a weapon I absolutely loved for its reliability. I still do.

Mid-morning, and after one or two lessons, we'd have a break and need little encouragement to go over to the NAAFI, an organization well known to anyone in the Armed Forces. It runs shops, canteens, launderettes and supermarkets on military bases. From there we'd get some milk to slurp and maybe scoff a pie for the extra calories before the next lesson.

As the exhausting days wore on, it soon became clear that our instructors loved messing us about. It started with the punishingly early mornings and continued as they jiggered with the itinerary. We'd have a lesson scheduled at 1 p.m. and due to last forty minutes, except that they'd suddenly slot in another lesson at 1.42 p.m., giving us just two minutes to get to it and putting us under extra pressure because woe betide you if you were late. *Drop and give me twenty. Faster! Too slow! Another five.*

In the afternoon, there would be more lessons and more fitness – usually some running. Never has one group of men run so much. We did everything at a sprint. If we crossed from one side of the square to the other, we did it at the double, and if you were last . . .

Drop and give me twenty.

FASTER.

The screaming and shouting. For a lot of the guys, this was a real culture shock. Many of the recruits just weren't used to being yelled at. You'd see grown men, eyes brimming with tears, just because they weren't accustomed to that kind of treatment.

One day, a member of our platoon, Wayne the Duke (answers on a postcard as to how he got that nickname), as worn raw by fatigue as the rest of us, asked the question: Why? Why do we have such late nights, and why are we up so early in the morning?

'You want more time in bed in the morning, do you?' barked Throb.

'No, Staff. But . . .'

'What is our motto?'

'Our . . .?'

'What is our fucking motto, Private?'

'Utrinque Paratus, Staff.'

You'll hear me say this phrase a lot: *it was drummed into us.* That motto was a prime example.

'And what does it stand for?'

'It stands for *Ready for Anything*, Staff.'

'Ready for anything as long as it happens during normal working hours, is it?'

'No, Staff.'

'No, because this is not a nine-to-five job,' bawled Throb. 'You want that, there's the fuckin' door. You're in the Army. More than that, you're a fuckin' Para, and if you're on an operation in the

Middle East or Northern Ireland, you're working until the early hours of the morning – three, four in the morning, say. Then something happens, and you're up again by five. There's a very good possibility that you'll be working twenty-four hours a day, and that's soldiering, and it's our job to prepare you for that. *Do I make myself fuckin' clear?'*

'Yes, Staff!'

Wayne the Duke didn't ask many more questions after that.

I was lucky. I already had grit when I came to the Regiment. I brought it with me from Sheffield, which is a hard city. I did my growing up during the era of football violence. Hooligans were responsible for the downturn of the game in this country and they were certainly responsible for giving me a tough childhood because it was tribal in Sheffield. Totally fierce. Whether you were a hoolie or not (I wasn't), you were still dragged into that world. You'd have to defend yourself every now and then. And that meant having to prove yourself.

It was that attitude and outlook that I'd packed along with my toothbrush when I set out for Depot. And one of the things I'd end up taking from that period – and moving forward from SAS selection too – is that if you want to prove yourself, there's no better way of doing it than by joining the military. I'll tell that to anyone – and I do. I meet a lot of guys who like to talk about how tough they are, dropping details of a misspent youth into the chat, but to them, I'll say, 'Go join the Paras and then train for the SAS. You'll find out how tough you really are.'

And if that sounds big-headed, fair enough. But I went there, and I know you need that kind of gumption to make it through. Every day of Para training was tough. But it wasn't about chest-forward boasting, shouting about how tough you are. It was about being tough. It wasn't about telling everyone how much you wanted it. It was about *showing* it. You'll have heard the expression 'actions speak louder than words'. It counts for double in the military. Treble in the Paras.

If it sounds like I very quickly 'got' the army, it's because I did. What the corporal said made sense and maybe even Wayne the Duke was satisfied with his answer. But, to me, it was like the question hardly needed asking. I didn't need to be told why we were ousted from our beds and into beastings at ungodly hours. I just got that we did. I could feel the effect it was having on me. A change. A change for the better.

Back to our day . . . After lunch, it might be a shorter run, say five miles or so, then more fieldcraft lessons. They mixed it up and every day would be a different combination of everything: classroom work, fitness drills, weapons training. They used to try to work it so that the particularly exhausting physical exercise took place at the end of the day – just so you weren't nodding off in lessons.

I'll come to weapons training later. For camouflage and concealment, we learned about the five S's of camouflage: shape, shine, shadow, silhouette, and spacing and movement. We were taught to ensure that we always broke up the line of the body so an observer wouldn't see a 'human' shape, as well as making sure that any shiny surfaces were hidden, maybe with mud, which you'd also use for your face.

I remember one particular exercise when we got to leave the classroom and go outside in order to spot several things hidden in long grass. A saucepan was one of them. You looked for an unusual shape, a shine, a different colour. And you needed to watch the position of the sun in order that you didn't cast a shadow.

At the end of the day, we'd usually do something especially gruelling – the assault course, perhaps, or a long run in order that we'd be sent to the cookhouse ravenous and exhausted. If they really wanted to mess with our heads, they'd schedule an evening lecture or something equally evil so that we wouldn't be crawling back to the block until much later. Other times, there might be a night exercise scheduled. We'd have what they called a 'night navex', the idea being to put some of the map-reading lessons into practice. They'd stick us in a Bedford four-tonner, take us to the training area and get us to practise our map skills.

Likewise, they'd often take advantage of bad weather. It's one thing learning about soldiering in a classroom or on a nice sunny day. Cooking food in the kitchen is easy. But cooking it outside? In a storm? Virtually every aspect of soldiering is more difficult in bad weather: eating, sleeping, firing a weapon.

It's a similar story with concealment. It might be a relatively simple matter to stay hidden for a short time, but doing it over an extended period, again in varied and difficult weather conditions, is much harder. You must stay concealed but still get on with the day-to-day. You'll need to map-read, eat, use the toilet.

About 5 p.m., we'd finish, have a massive dinner at the cookhouse and then start on our evening block jobs and/or homework or – after we'd checked the schedule – preparation for the next day. Pretty quickly, I'd worked out that it was best to do as much as possible the night before and I got into the habit of making sure that the kit needed for the next day (they'd post a kit list as part of the itinerary each evening) was washed and ironed. I also made a point of having my shower and shave last thing.

In the mornings, some of my fellow recruits (looking at you, Wayne the Duke) would run around like headless chickens, late for breakfast and in some cases stinting on it (for which they'd pay later when it came to running) before a dash back to the block to do their jobs.

But for me, it was all about getting ready ahead of time, which is another lesson I've retained to this day. We had a saying in the army: Prior Preparation and Planning Prevents Piss-Poor Performance, which speaks for itself, and I took it to heart. Even having prepared the night before, I'd still get up an hour before most of the other Toms to avoid the rush and jostle for the same few basins with fifty other guys, to make sure I didn't forget things, didn't make mistakes and didn't rush my food. These are the kind of circumstances that breed errors and even injury.

Still, all that prep took time. Some nights, I'd still be awake and working at 2 a.m., knowing I only had three or four hours of sleep before it all started again. Plenty of others were the same. It was the reason recruits started to leave, sometimes at the rate of three or four a week. It was the relentlessness of it all. You'd do a day, think *That was hard*, and then must do it again the next day and the day after that. Again, an early morning and punishing physical exercise. Again, the cold and the wet and the dirt. Again, getting screamed at and insulted by instructors.

I saw blokes who'd started out as keen as mustard just . . . *wilt*. I saw the fire and light slowly go out of their eyes. The next thing you knew, they were packing a bag, or you'd look around one day and there'd be an empty bed.

THE TAKEAWAY

Like we say: Do the basics well. Joining the Army, it stood me in good stead that I came from a houseproud family where my mum in particular kept things running like clockwork. I didn't realize it at the time, of course, but she was a model of efficiency. When I joined up, the procedures of a tidy room, tidy dress, tidy locker layout and tidy living area were normal to me. My mum had made me 'house efficient'. As a result, I was showing guys how to iron shirts, polish boots, put a crease in their trousers.

'Why?' was the question. What was the point of all this relentless spick-and-spanning? Firstly, it was to bring us all up to the same (high) standards. Secondly, I learned in life that nothing is done without order or structure and that it starts with being organized and tidy. As soon as there's a breakdown in that order, you find things don't function as well. So, if you can be structured and ordered and tidy within your block (or home), it will spill over into your life in the field (or work, or family life etc.).

CHAPTER 4

LIVING AN ARDUOUS LIFE

'We must all suffer from one of two pains: the pain of discipline or the pain of regret. The difference is discipline weighs ounces while regret weighs tons'

– Jim Rohn

Years ago, while serving with the Regiment (and when I say Regiment, by the way, I mean the SAS), I was working with Mountain Troop in the Arctic. It was a particularly evil night: we were stuck halfway up a hostile mountain with temperatures 40-below, and we'd been hiking all day and most of the evening. A blizzard had come up, so we were keen to get under cover, eat and recover from what had been a tough day.

Pitching tents was hard as around us the wind increased and visibility went down to near zero. Snow stuck to our goggles and seemed to penetrate our outerwear. Even wearing state-of-the-art mountain troop gear, we wouldn't last long in weather like this. We worked hard and fast until, eventually, with the tents up, I was ready to clamber inside.

But was stopped.

'*Huh?*'

There's a technique Mountain Troop use. They pack the outside base of the tent with snow, almost igloo-like, to make sure it can't whisk up and blow away.

'Sorry, Des, we've got to do it.' My guide sounded rueful as he shouted to be heard above the blizzard that howled around us.

There was maybe half a second when I thought *Really? Do we have to?* After all, one of the lads had said he thought the wind was dropping. Couldn't we take the risk? Maybe climb inside, rest up a bit, get warmer, and *then* do it?

Instead, something kicked in and I nodded and set to the task of packing the tents with snow.

As it turned out, it was worth doing. The blizzard, far from blowing out, only intensified, and as my buddy pointed out, there was every chance that we'd have to pull ourselves from our sleeping bags, emerge into the maelstrom and pack the tents with snow anyway.

That 'thing' that kicked in? It's called discipline.

It was Mike Tyson who said that discipline is doing what you hate doing but nonetheless doing it like you love it. He didn't like training. He didn't like getting up at 5 a.m. and going for a five-mile run. But he did it anyway. According to him, that was why he won fights. That discipline brought him success.

For him, of course, success came in the ring. Me, I have to look back at my military career. Knowing I've worked to protect my country and therefore, in some small way, safeguarded the freedoms we all enjoy is a feeling of having succeeded in life. It hasn't brought me riches or heavyweight championships, but it's brought me fulfilment. It's helped me to (and I know it sounds corny but . . .) 'find myself'.

It began almost from the moment I stepped into Depot back in May 1977. For a start, I realized I was a lot brighter than I'd thought I was. I didn't have a qualification to my name, but during Basic, I learned I had a lot of what you might call common sense. I learned that I was able to adapt to a system and make the system work for me. I developed a sense of knowing when to use my initiative and when to blindly follow orders, and I realized that blindly following orders often required using my initiative.

Further down the line, and also thanks to the military, I would become somebody I thought of as being educated, somebody who was technically proficient, somebody who could speak several languages.

At the root of all the personal success I've enjoyed are the principles of hard work, consistency, focus and discipline. They speak for themselves, but of them all, discipline is the most important because if you don't have that, you can't have the rest. I firmly believe that the more disciplined you are, the better soldier you are. And I believe that the better soldier you are, the better human being you have the potential to be.

Wayne the Duke wasn't the only guy to question the levels of discipline we were expected to maintain during our CIC. Lockers tidy, boots polished, block gleaming, beds made a certain way. What did that have to do with engaging an enemy in combat?

First, we were told that standards were high in barracks because they'd drop in the field. 'Your standards will fall,' we were told, 'but they'll never fall lower than anyone else's.'

Another thing: discipline is a creed, a way of being. So, no, in the field, you won't be polishing your boots or keeping a locker tidy, but you will be practising discipline and that'll kick in when you're cold and wet and would rather do anything than strip and clean your weapon but do it anyway. Or when you're desperate to shelter from a blizzard, but you need to strengthen your tent. It's doing what you hate but doing it anyway.

In fact, in the field, you'll need to be even more disciplined than when inside the barracks because you're not trying to avoid a gobful from Throb and his mates, you're trying not to get killed. The bullshit is the barracks, but it also serves you when you're out in the field, when you're fighting both enemy and weather.

While in the Paras, I came to realize that discipline was paramount in everything that I did – a life of discipline lived every day. I formulated a series of certain things that I did every day and still do.

The first one is to *get up early*, don't lie around in bed, and *get your jobs done*. You should get as much sleep as you can, seven to eight hours if possible. But once you've had your sleep, drag yourself out of your pit and do your work. Don't leave anything until tomorrow that can be done today. Remember those late-night block jobs done when I wanted nothing more than to climb into bed? The preparation I did for the following day? Both were, in part, responsible for getting me through Basic.

Next, *do some physical*. I don't care what it is or when. But get some exercise. I truly believe that by keeping yourself fit, healthy and in shape, you're taking steps to success. It's good for your body and great for your mental health. And it means you can have the odd KitKat without feeling guilty.

Another one: *eat healthily*. Your body cannot function unless you have the right nutrients. In the military, ration packs are calorie-dense to keep you going. Outside the military, healthy, nutritious food and plenty of water is the key.

Next, *think of your mind*. It's your body's partner and you need to look after it. Do what you need to do, be that praying, meditating, practising mindfulness or setting goals for yourself. Added to this, I'd say read. In the military, you can always be reading something, whether it's orders, instructions or, later in my case, educating myself on language and local customs for working on the ground in the SAS. Whatever you're reading, let it be something that feeds your mind. Let it be nutrition for your brain, just as food is nutrition for your body.

Next, *cleanliness*. That's clean yourself, clean your living area. It's important for health and hygiene reasons. In the field, you must keep clean and dry to avoid foot rot, skin rashes and all manner of other unpleasant things. Often, you'll need to wash when you least want to do it, when you simply want to curl up in a sleeping bag. This is where the discipline comes in. You do it even though you don't want to. If you don't, you'll pay for it later.

And that's it. They're the principles I live by. They first began to provide a foundation for my life back in Para training and have done ever since. I think that, by following this creed, I've found happiness or whatever you want to call it. Fulfilment. Contentment. Abiding by them, I've worked my way into the Paras and then into the SAS, and I've done things money can't buy.

But the important thing is that, although I began as a recruit when I had something to work towards, I've continued as a man into his sixties. I live an arduous life because even though in the short-term it might be hard, it brings rewards in the long-term.

Leading on from that, I guess you could say it was fortuitous that the Paras and I found each other. We were often told that the Paras was the most disciplined regiment and, with years of military service behind me, I can exclusively reveal that they weren't lying. We were the guys who punched a hole in the enemy and, to do that, the army needed a soldier who was harder and more well-drilled than the usual crap hat. That was the regime. Some people took to it (guilty). Others didn't.

THE TAKEAWAY

I think I've said enough for this bit, don't you?

CHAPTER 5

TACTICAL ADVANCE TO BATTLE

'I can bear any pain as long as it has meaning'
– Haruki Murakami

Bang.

It would happen at a moment's notice. We'd be in our block doing whatever we were doing when the corporals would burst in unannounced, faces even harder than usual, probably carrying clipboards.

'Listen up. We want you in the corridor now,' came the cry, and we knew to leave whatever we'd been doing. Whatever we were wearing, even if it was just underpants, even naked, God forbid, we had to come running that very second.

'Right,' bellowed Throb. 'I can see that this floor is dirty.' He indicated a floor that sparkled, a floor you could have eaten your dinner off. 'Right. Down. Give me twenty.'

Press-ups, of course. Press-ups were the standard punishment for most infractions, but as I was about to learn, they had a few tricks up their sleeve. Another instructor returned from having inspected the shower area. Consulting his clipboard, he said, 'Smith and Clark, you were down for cleaning the showers. The showers are clean. But Powell, what the fuck have you done with those sinks?'

I'd cleaned the sinks to within an inch of their lives. But it didn't matter. I was summoned forward and handed a bumper. A bumper is a big heavy block with felt on the underside. You put liquid polish on the floor and swipe the bumper from side to side to clean the floor. You've likely seen them used before.

'Powell, you thick northern twat. Do you know the bumper test, Powell?'

I shook my head. 'No, Staff.'

'Kneel there, back to the wall.'

I did as told and was handed a bumper. 'Right, hold the bumper.'

This is the bumper test, I thought, holding the bumper, which was heavy but not that heavy. *I can handle this.*

'Hold it still, Powell, hold it still.'

After about a minute, it began to hurt. And then *really* hurt.

'Can you see him quivering?' barked Throb. 'The oxygen is going to his brain, taking it away from his muscles. He's from Sheffield, so he's not used to oxygen in his brain, are you, Powell? Keep going, Powell.'

I held it until I could do so no longer and had to drop it, much to Throb's disgust.

Occasionally, they'd lighten things up a bit. On the day of my twentieth birthday, we ended a run with me climbing the few steps to the cookhouse and standing there like a turkey as the lads serenaded me with 'Happy Birthday'.

Another time, we were out running on the tank tracks. Located in Aldershot's Long Valley, the tank tracks were exactly that:

huge parallel ditches of churned-up mud into which water had collected. A few times a week, we'd have to run the dreaded 'tank tracks', navigating the uneven terrain and enduring the discomfort of the wet and cold. On one occasion, we reached an area where there was a large, steep mound. 'Right, Powell,' said Boil. 'Do they have moving pictures where you're from? Have the movies got that far north yet?'

'Yes, Staff.'

'Ooh, very la-di-da. And have you seen the *Rocky* film?'

'Yes, Staff.'

'Are you speaking Northern to me, Powell, you thick pie-eating twat? Speak the Queen's English.'

'Sorry, Staff.'

'Right, I want you to run to the top of that mound just like in the *Rocky* film, have you got that?'

'Yes, Staff.'

Reaching the top, I was ordered to 'do a Rocky' and pranced around waving my hands in the air just like Sylvester Stallone in the movie – much to the delight of everybody standing down below.

'All right, stop your laughing,' came the outraged response. 'What are you doing messing about like that, Powell, you gobby northern twat? Get back down here right now.'

'Yes, Staff.' You didn't bother arguing, pointing out that you were just doing exactly as you'd been ordered to do. You were doing a Rocky. There was no point because by then I understood the instructors' role in life – a role they took to with gusto – was that of mind-fuckers. And conflicting orders were all part of the package.

But – and I can't emphasize this enough – that was me. *I got it.* I was that bit older and probably came into training with the right kind of mindset, a mindset that helped me survive.

Plenty didn't. Like I say, recruits had started dropping off almost from day one. Some left because they picked up an injury (although they might be 'backsquadded', which meant they could heal up and then join the recruit company behind us – 440 Platoon in our case).

There were also those who simply never reached the required level of fitness. We didn't know it at the time, but training had been structured to improve our fitness in increments. That beasting we had on the first day felt like hell, but that's because we were unfit. As we improved, they began taking us outside, first running in plimsolls, then in boots. Running three miles, then five, until eventually, by the time of P Company, we'd be doing ten-mile tabs carrying all the gear.

But although some of us came into training relatively fit (again, guilty as charged), others needed more work to get up to speed. That meant going on runs and spending a bit of time in the gym. But to give up your spare time took the kind of focus, discipline and drive I'm talking about. Some didn't have it.

And then there was the abuse. The punishments and press-ups. The constant threat of getting reprimanded if something wasn't right. During any given day, you'd expect half a dozen clips around the ear, digs in your side, even a little punch just to keep you on your toes. And I know it wouldn't happen nowadays, but this was the 1970s which, as anyone who lived through that period knows, was a different, more feral time with far fewer concessions to political correctness than there are now. Recruits were yelled at, sworn at, belittled and insulted. I got stick for being from the north. But, say, if you had a big nose, you'd expect to get called 'beaky' or 'Pinocchio'. Your ears stuck out? 'Pick up the pace, you jug-eared bastard.' And if you were carrying a few extra pounds? Don't get me started.

'If you don't straighten that fucking arm, I will break it and reset it, do you understand me?' Even if you have the life experience to know an empty threat when you hear one, it's still violent and intimidating. To a kid who's never been away from home, it lands differently. I'd see the younger ones quail. There were those who found it harder to take than others, but no quarter was given. Every recruit got the same treatment and it was on a spectrum of 'harsh' at one end and 'very harsh' at the other, all of it not only tolerated but expected by command.

For many of the recruits, it could be a vicious circle. If an instructor thought you weren't pulling your weight, then he'd come down on you hard, and the harder he came down on you, the worse it got. You'd get picked on, taken outside and told to do pull-ups on the metal girders that linked the blocks, or ordered to get down and do twenty press-ups. The more of that you did, the more tired you got, and the more tired you got, the more mistakes you made.

There was one incident where some of the guys had been marching on a second square parallel to a perimeter road open to the public. An old lady walking her dogs had heard a load of fruity language and put in a complaint, which obviously fed back to the instructors.

It wasn't the bad language she objected to; it was the derogatory nature of the comments. I'll leave it to your imagination as to what kind of comments they might have been. Of course, this came back down from command, but it was never a case of 'Don't speak to the recruits like that' – just a case of 'Don't let members of the public hear you talking to recruits like that.'

And although this was exactly the kind of thing that gave the Regiment its fearsome reputation, it was too much for some of the recruits. It didn't happen in my platoon, but there were countless stories of guys going AWOL. I even heard tales of past recruits who'd killed themselves. One guy apparently went up to the range, put the barrel of a rifle in his mouth and pulled the trigger.

When it became wider public knowledge that this sort of thing used to go on (funnily enough, about the same time that the army tried to stamp it out), people used to say to me, 'But didn't you disagree with all that, Des?' To be honest, the answer was always no, I didn't. To me, it was part of training – and an important part, because if training had been easy, I wouldn't have wanted to do it. I wanted to challenge and push myself. I wanted to be dragged out of my comfort zone. For me, that was half the appeal. You don't get hard by being treated soft.

Even so, it's why so many fell by the wayside. At the end of the day, they learned something about themselves: they learned either that they didn't have the desire or that their desire wasn't as great as they thought. Basic training will weed out anybody not serious about wanting to be in the Regiment. They'll naturally fail.

Why? For a start, it's hard, so if you don't want it, you're not going to get it. Secondly, instructors are looking at you, assessing you the whole time, and they'll spot anybody who treats the whole thing like a joke, who doesn't pull their weight, who shirks jobs in the block, who tries to cut corners when it comes to fitness. Something will be said. Either way, the system weeds out those who are not suited to the Regiment.

Because Scouse and I were that little bit older than other recruits, the corporals used us a bit, giving us the responsibility of maybe having a quiet word if a recruit wasn't working hard enough, helping a younger guy who might be struggling with something. You've probably seen the movies where the guys get fed up with one recruit holding them back. *Full Metal Jacket*, for example, or *A Few Good Men*. We never got as far as putting bars of soap in socks, but that's not to say we'd be happy carrying other Toms. You'd have a word. 'Come on, pull your socks up. Get a grip.' Nobody wants their fellow soldiers giving them the side-eye, wondering if they can be trusted to pull their weight. A word or two was usually all it took.

One lad, Gaz, was always trying to get home at the weekend to see his girlfriend. Either that or he'd be on the payphone calling her. And call me old-fashioned, but if you join the military, you're going to be away from home a lot. For the first six weeks, we didn't go on leave at all. Weekends would be spent washing kit, ironing it, getting ready for Monday. I think it was after the first eight weeks that we had a weekend off. After that, at every opportunity, Gaz was off.

Which meant that, soon, Gaz was off permanently, one of the many to drop off in the first three or four months. There were lots of those. There were plenty who decided they couldn't hack it for one reason or another.

Remember Wayne the Duke? He thought it was funny to lounge around on his bed while others got on with their block jobs. He went as well. I can't remember if it was of his own accord or if he was told to leave, but I do recall it was no great surprise. Rarely was an absence mourned. Sometimes the opposite. We were just glad to be rid of the dead wood. We appreciated the fact that the more competent we got, the less of a bollocking we got from the instructors.

Meanwhile, we were introduced to the art of tabbing. Tab is an acronym which stands for 'tactical advance to battle' and is basically done at half-doubling, half-marching pace while carrying full weight, which would be a weapon, and our pack called a Bergen. ('Tabbing' and 'yomping' are the same thing, by the way. It's just that tabbing is a Para term and yomping used by Marines.)

Tabbing is central to the whole ethos of the Regiment, its entire reason for being. A paratrooper is an airborne-trained soldier expected to jump out of an aircraft, hit the ground hard, tab to battle, and fight. They're spearhead troops, ready for action at a moment's notice.

On runs, we would generally do five or ten miles with boots on. When it came to tabbing, we would be doing the same distance but with Bergen, weapon and crash hat. We'd be expected to go over the assault course carrying full kit up to a weight of 35 pounds, which is almost 16 kilograms. All of this was taking us up to P Company, the pre-parachute selection test which, if you wanted to be a paratrooper, you had to pass.

P Company had first been introduced in the 1940s and was not a test of soldiering skills. That happened as we went along. It was more about challenging our spirit, testing our fitness and stamina. It was about finding out if you had the guts to be a paratrooper. Do you have the drive, desire, will and determination? Are you prepared to go that extra mile? Are you the guy who can charge at an enemy?

P Company consisted of eight separate tests which would take place over four or five days. They were . . .

DAY ONE

Trainasium

We've been through this one, right? A test of balance and confidence, they have you running into nets, they have you walking on uneven bars. As we said, the trainasium's a bottle test designed to see if you're willing to jump out of an aircraft at height. Traditionally, it was the first of the P Company tests. It was the only one that was a straight pass or fail; you were awarded points on the other events. In other words, if you couldn't hack the trainasium, then you might as well grab your travel pass and be on the next train out of Aldershot.

Ten-Mile Battle March, aka 'The Ten-Miler'

With our SLRs and the Bergen rucksack packed to a weight of 35lbs, we'd have to tab ten miles in two hours. The point of tabbing was to keep pace with the rest of the company, so if everybody else was half-doubling, then that's what you did. Of course, in reality – and certainly in a test situation like P

Company – you'd soon spread out. Our job was to reach certain checkpoints and complete the entire march in one hour and fifty minutes – and certainly no more than two hours, which would be a fail.

The run took place around the training areas close to the barracks, which incorporated several different terrains: heathland, woodland, lots of sand and grit, and, of course, the treacherous tank tracks of Long Valley.

Unfortunately for us, there had been plenty of rain in the weeks leading up to P Company, so those tank traps were at their stinking muddiest, with chewed-up mud and horrible-looking yellow pools. (Why yellow? I don't know.) I'd seen recruits lose boots in those pools on runs and I dearly hoped that neither the stretcher race nor the long log race would involve them. (We didn't know beforehand because, with the exception of the trainasium and steeplechase, we didn't train or practise for P Company at all.)

DAY TWO

The Log Race

The feared log race. Just as the final day's stretcher race would mimic a retreat with casualties, the log race aimed to simulate carrying the barrel of a gun. Each log, weighing 60kg, was carried by eight men over a distance of 1.9 miles.

Steeplechase

The steeplechase was another event with which we had some experience. It was a 1.8-mile cross-country course that involved running over hurdles and through rivers dressed in PT kit and boots. To pass, you had to complete it in fewer than nineteen minutes.

DAY THREE

The Two-Miler

Like the ten-miler, except this one was to be done at a sprint and without a Bergen. For the two-miler, we had to be what they call 'battle ready', which meant weapon, crash hat and webbing, the idea being that you were running to the front line to fight.

Assault Course

Three circuits of the assault course in fewer than seven minutes and thirty seconds.

DAY FOUR

The Stretcher Race

In teams of sixteen over a course of five miles, we would have to race carrying a steel stretcher weighing 175lbs. The idea was that the weight of the stretcher should mimic that of a casualty, and the race itself approximate a retreat with an injury. A stretcher only has four carriers, with other team members running behind, then changing at intervals, which is exactly what would happen, all things being equal.

As the name suggests, it was a race. The team that completed seven and a half miles first was the winner, but that didn't necessarily mean each stretcher bearer was automatically graded accordingly. Instructors would be watching for those recruits who pulled their weight and those who might have let others pick up the slack. It was perfectly possible to be on the winning team and still fail, and vice versa. The same applied to . . .

Milling

Milling was perhaps the oddest and most feared of the tests. The basic idea was that you and another recruit had to stand in front of each other and fight for a minute straight. It was a test of sheer blood and guts, one where you weren't allowed to fade or shirk from the task at hand. You just had to fight. They called it the longest minute.

We were told there'd be plenty of recruits who wouldn't complete some of these tasks, particularly the ten-miler, and that the stretcher race and log races usually claimed a few victims as well. Thanks to the points system – and apart from the trainasium – it would be possible to fail at one task but still pass P Company if you had excelled in other areas. Fall too far behind, though, and you'd either be backsquadded or out on your ear.

THE TAKEAWAY

It was Thomas Jefferson who said, 'I'm a great believer in luck, and I find the harder I work the more I have of it.' The golfer Gary Player put it even more succinctly. 'The harder I work, the luckier I get.'

Hard work is what I want to talk about. Nothing of any merit was ever achieved without it. Hard work breeds familiarity: the harder you work, the easier things become.

I also discovered that in the military, if you worked hard, you got a payback: you got fitter, your instructors wouldn't pick on you and you improved at whatever it was you were doing.

I can't emphasize it enough. Hard work reaps its own rewards.

CHAPTER 6

P COMPANY

"The road to every kingdom travels through hostile territory'
– Eddie Pinero

The eight logs, each about half the length of a telegraph pole and maybe twice the circumference, lay in the middle of the wet and muddy track. And although they were just logs modified with toggles for carrying, to me, they looked more foreboding than that. They looked like ... I don't know, sharks or something. Something bad anyway.

We, the P Company few, stood some yards away. We were doing warm-ups. Not because we were especially athletic, but because it was cold and we literally wanted to warm up.

And, of course, we were at the tank tracks. The dreaded tank tracks. It would have to be. They were hard enough to run in webbing, let alone while harnessed to a heavy log. And they weren't quite wide enough to accommodate teams of six, which meant there'd be a lot of jockeying for position when the race began.

As with most tests in P Company, we had no experience of the log race, the reason being you didn't practise P Company. You didn't rehearse or have dry runs (*dry* run – as if). We knew the assault course and trainasium, of course, and we'd done a hell of a lot of running. But the log race, the stretcher race and the milling were all new to us.

Of these three, it was the log race that had filled me with the greatest trepidation. I wasn't sure why. Just that from what we'd been told, it sounded especially hard. That toggle, for example. It locked on your wrist, so if you slipped and fell, you either dragged down the rest of your team – and would suffer the verbal abuse accordingly – or were likely to get your arm yanked out of its socket as the other guys ploughed on. Was it that? I don't know. Just something about it. Some unknown and intimidating element not present with, say, the stretcher race or even the milling, which the majority of the lads were most worried about.

For me, it was this one. A brutally hard race, we had been told. A physically demanding test that would also draw on your reserves of mental strength. They were just words, though. We still had no idea what to expect. And even now, with the logs laid out ahead of us, things weren't much clearer.

We'd been split into teams of six per log, wearing boots, denims, red PT vests and helmets.

'Listen up,' came the shout. 'When we blow the whistle, you run, get on a log and run with it until you reach the endpoint. You got that?'

'Yes, Staff,' we all yelled together.

'Three, two, one, *go*.'

Herded together in a group, grim-faced and determined, we all began pounding towards our chosen weapons of torture.

The P Company tests were presided over by instructors drafted in for that very purpose. They were the reason that numbers had been painted on our helmets. We were not names to them, just numbers, the idea being that they'd have no preconceptions about us. It wasn't a case of our regular instructors having favourites – the very idea was laughable – more that our usual corporals would have preconceptions. They'd know which of us could do what. Who was strongest, who was weakest.

The other thing was that we'd been joined by a second group of soldiers known as the All-Arms Company. This lot were already trained troops but came from a variety of different regiments – Marines, Engineers, Signallers, Guardsmen and so on. What they had in common was a desire to get their wings. If you wanted to be a parachutist in the British Army, whatever your regiment, you had to pass P Company, and to do that, you needed to first undergo a two-and-a-half-week build-up process and then join the current recruit company at Aldershot (nowadays it's Catterick).

By that stage, there were around twenty to thirty of us left in the recruit company, and we were joined by another thirty or so All-Arms guys.

So the race began – and with it the shouting. Not only were the newly arrived P Company instructors shouting at us, but we had Throb, Boil and Cpl Smith with us too, screaming abuse or encouragement, depending on your perspective.

First thing: get a good grip on the toggle. It's not like you can ask the guys to stop while you sort yourself out. You must keep on going. Whatever happens, you must keep on going.

We reached our log. My hand went through the toggle, which

gripped my wrist tight. On a count of 'one, two, three', we all lifted together and . . .

My God, it was heavy. We'd been told that it was going to feel like wild horses pulling you apart and whoever said that wasn't wrong. As we set off, pain flared almost straightaway and, with it, the knowledge that there was no stopping to rest or adjust, no quick-pausing to change arms. This was it. This was it for the next mile and a half. The volume increased. Men shouting with effort and pain. Mud-splashed faces screwed up.

'That's it, good pace. Get the pace right, guys, let's get it going.'

The pace. Because we were all so inextricably linked, getting the pace right was very important indeed. To do that, you needed to work as a team. You needed to listen to the man next to you and trust that he was listening to you.

Ahead of us, we had one and a half miles of wet and muddy terrain to negotiate with our log, the objective being to ideally come in first but, most especially, not come in last. Coming in last meant the six of you being borderline, needing to over-perform elsewhere or face possible failure.

As we ran, the instructors continued to cajole, urging us forward. Behind us, other instructors were doing the same with the team at our heels. 'You're not going to let them beat you, are you? That lot? That bunch of no-marks?'

'Come on. Come on. Do you want to be a paratrooper? Do you want to be a paratrooper or not?'

I don't know what it was like for others. Perhaps the physical hardship reduced their desire. For me, it sharpened it. It pushed me on. Was I going to go through all of this for nothing? All those pitch-black morning runs and midnight finishes. The cold and wet. The abuse. The constant sniffling with cold symptoms because your immune system is so weakened by permanent exhaustion.

Was I going to go through all that and fail?

No.

The team to our left began to pull ahead. They'd managed to find a pace that worked for them and knew it. They were playing the advantage for all it was worth.

In second place, we weren't doing too badly, but as the team ahead put a yard or so between them and us, our boots began to slide on the mud they'd freshly churned.

Behind us, a team urged on by an instructor was practically nudging us. One of their lads was being especially gobby, screaming and shouting at the other team members, encouraging them until they drew to the side of us and began to nose ahead. They had slightly overplayed it, though, and paid for the burst of strength when one of them lost his footing, slid, fell to his knees and slowed the others down. We surged past their temporarily stopped log – back into second place.

Then it was my turn to fall. For a moment, I went to one knee and must have hit a rock because pain lanced up my thigh from my knee. I'd pay for that later, but for the time being, it didn't matter. All I cared about was getting up quick and, although the log lurched and I was subject to a barrage of insults, no time was lost. As we reached a hill, the guy behind me slid and both his legs went from under him. This time it was my turn to launch a volley of abuse as we all screamed at him to get up.

Ahead of us loomed the hill and the team behind pushed past us, literally shouldering us out of the way, screaming venom at us, getting it back in return. We threw ourselves at the hill. Any thoughts of being cold were long, long gone. We were red-hot now, steam coming off every one of us as we threw ourselves up the slope like men possessed, yelling with the pain and the struggle, hands and wrists blistered by the toggle rope but not caring. We were concentrating only on getting the log to its berth.

Those behind us struggled even more. They were in our slip-stream, having to deal with the mud churned up not just by our boots, but also by the boots of the team in front. They were well ahead now, the outright winners unless something went terribly wrong. The real struggle was here in second place. The instructors knew it too and many seemed to have gathered around us now that the titanic struggle was nearing its end. The team behind were screaming and yelling and, in a gargantuan effort, made it to the top of the hill right on our heels. Along the tank tracks, we could see the endpoint and it gave us a lift. We weren't listening to the instructors now. We weren't heeding the shouts and insults from behind either. All we cared about was reaching the chequered flag and getting there ahead of the team behind, but mainly . . .

. . . not carrying this godforsaken instrument of pain.

In many ways, the log race was a perfect representation of what P Company was all about. I often say of the SAS that it churns out a certain type of person. You can't teach a guy to excel in violence and then expect him to lead a normal life. This is also true of the Paras. A Para – that punch-a-hole-in-the-enemy soldier – is a soldier who must rush forward. You can't have a quiet guy do that. This is why Paras often get into trouble on civvy nights out. It's because the Parachute Regiment training is geared towards creating loud, aggressive soldiers, soldiers who are trained to kill and not to be community-minded. This is a major, major difference with the SAS where so much of what we did was based around hearts and minds.

It's a philosophy that takes it out on your body. It's no surprise that I have metal hips now. No surprise that most of my friends have bad backs, bad knees, bad necks. No surprise that they're all limping. You can't go through that kind of training and not get injured, not be affected.

As it happens, I've skipped ahead. The first day of training P Company was the dreaded trainasium. Now, this was the one test where we had some practice, mainly because it was so dangerous. There isn't a lot to say about it other than there's a lot of crabbing along its scaffolding poles at various heights and a run-and-jump carried out at about 30 metres off the ground – another of the army's beloved bottle tests.

Years later, working as a PT instructor, I was showing some recruits a bottle test similar to the trainasium – trying to demonstrate the technique whereby you hurl yourself off the platform and into the net, punching through to grab it. Embarrassingly, I got it wrong, missed and only just managed to grab the bottom of the net in time to not exactly break my fall but at least absorb some of the impact. As it was, I lay on the floor winded with the trainees looking on.

'I'm all right, I'm all right,' I managed as they shuffled over to find out if I was still alive. But, God, it hurt.

That was from a height of around 10 feet. From 30? That's a different matter. We would often have guys on that bit of kit who simply couldn't do it. One of the jumps was a bit of an optical illusion. When you were up there, it looked far wider than it was. You had to take that fact on trust as you launched yourself off the scaffold and a lot of guys couldn't do that.

We also had a guy who fell. Luckily, it was from one of the lower jumps, maybe 15 feet, but even so, not good. It was a sobering moment for the rest of us. That said, I seem to recall that nobody failed the trainasium which, considering it was our first test, was something of a relief.

Given what I've said about the point of the trainasium being to sniff out a fear of heights, it was encouraging that none of our would-be paratroopers failed at the first hurdle. That afternoon was the ten-mile tab.

For the ten-mile tab, instructors ran with us with packs on their backs but no weapons. Our instructors were guys who lived the arduous life. It was they who decided that the ideal time for the tab should be an hour and forty-five minutes because that was their time. Put it this way, for the rest of the British Army, the target was two hours, yet if we finished beyond two hours during P Company, then points would be deducted.

And it was brutal. Ten miles with 35lbs on your back. That's almost three stone in weight that you have to carry, along with water and weapon, maintaining a half-run/half-walking pace on a variety of different terrains. You've got the P Company instructors screaming at you. You've got the 439 Platoon instructors screaming at you. Every mile feels like twenty.

Some didn't make it to the end. Much to the disgust of the instructors, a day that had started with a 100 per cent pass rate on the trainasium suddenly took another turn.

The day after that was super-tough. We had the log race in the morning, followed by the steeplechase in the afternoon. As I've explained, the steeplechase is basically running through the woodland over jumps and wading through water. An obstacle race, basically. The individual obstacles are not difficult in themselves, but when it's one after another, then it's tough and it's exhausting. Coming on top of the previous physical exertion, it can almost break you.

At least we're not on the tank tracks, I thought as I got my head down and raced, feeling heart, lungs, muscles, everything aching.

The next day was the two-miler where we were equipped with weapons and webbing. The webbing is for survival kit. It's where you store your water bottles, extra ammo and such like. Obviously, it's not as brutal as having to tab with a Bergen, but the difference is that you must do the two miles at a sprint and you must complete the race in fewer than eighteen minutes or face being marked down.

Next up was the assault course, three times round. Even though we'd done it many times before during our training, this one was different. I liken it to a gymnast who practises their routine over and over, but on the day of the competition faces all that extra pressure. On this occasion, I remember being especially aware that it was important to get upfront quickly. Like the log race, those in front tend to have it a bit easier. For example, on the assault course is a move we called gate-vaulting. It's much easier to be the first guy up there because you're just vaulting over, whereas the guy behind must worry about getting kicked in the face.

It's the same with water obstacles. The guy in front has a clear field, but the one behind tends to get buffeted and channelled by the churned-up water. I managed it within the allotted time. And, for once, I didn't vomit. Next stop, the stretcher race.

The stretcher race involved four team members carrying the metal stretcher with four behind carrying the team's weapons. This made it slightly (keyword: *slightly*) less brutal than the log race, because at least you got the chance to swap over now and then. The problem arises if you have a taller Tom on one side, which can upset the balance. And, again, it's difficult when you get a team in front of you. I came off it with bad shoulders, grazed knees and bloodied elbows, and at one stage was bashed in the mouth by the metal frame, which had jumped up. But, as with the other tests, it was a case of showing guts and determination, a reminder that P Company and, by extension, Para training isn't just a case of being dead fit (for example, we've had Commonwealth athletes coming along and failing P Company). It's about having the right attitude and showing real true grit. That was clear throughout the few days, but if one test really exemplified it, then it was milling.

'We could teach your mother to be a soldier if we wanted,' was something often said. 'Any chump can fire a weapon. We can teach map-reading to anyone. But to be a paratrooper is different. Paratroopers are not mechanized. Para Reg is about blood and guts.'

And this is where milling came in. You had to stand toe-to-toe with another recruit and bash each other, which was less about being the toughest and much more about overcoming fear, about being the guy with the most grit.

I was hoping that my opponent might be a backsquadder or a

soldier from All-Arms. Some of those guys had been a bit arrogant prior to the tests beginning and although that hadn't lasted, the bad taste had lingered. So yeah, one of them, please.

Instead, I got a Tom from 439 called Jake, a bloke I got on with. Well, at least it wasn't Scouse.

'You're not going to use your kung fu on me, are you?' laughed Jake, who knew I'd been into martial arts prior to joining up.

But 'kung fu' was of no use here. They didn't want tactics. They wanted punches thrown as hard as possible for one minute. Besides which, my speciality was karate (First Dan, thank you very much).

'Right. In the middle, on a count of three. One, two, three, go.'

Wearing boxing gloves and face guards, we started going at each other, swinging as hard and as fast as possible like the worst most undisciplined pub fight you've ever seen.

Neither of us went down. I will say that. And no, I didn't use my 'kung fu' on him.

My back ached, my shoulders hurt and my knees and elbows were all scraped up, but to be honest, I knew I'd passed P Company. So when my name was read out, it wasn't any great surprise. The feeling was more of elation. Those who had failed – about thirteen lads – were told in the same matter-of-fact fashion as the rest of us had been told we'd passed. It came as no surprise to any of them either. Next for them would be a visit to our commanding officer where their future would be decided. Some would join the company coming up behind us. Some would return to civvy life. Others would try a different regiment.

Meanwhile, the rest of us were to get back to the block, clean it and get ready for Monday when training would continue. It wouldn't be long now before we'd go to Brize Norton, where parachute training would begin.

THE TAKEAWAY

I've spoken about the value of hard work and I'll be that way until the day I die. But as well as working hard, you must work smart. That means leaving enough in the tank to take it to the next level.

That was P Company. It was a series of tests designed to take us to the next level. It was about asking the same question of yourself that you should ask when you're in an especially challenging situation: How much do I want this?

There's a simple formula when it comes to answering that question. If you really want something, you'll work harder than ever before. You'll endure discomfort. You'll make sacrifices. You will give EVERYTHING. (Another saying, this one from the Para days: We will give everything if everything is what it takes.)

If you're not prepared to give everything, maybe you don't want that thing as much as you thought. And if you work hard but don't quite make the grade, at least you can say you worked as hard as you could. You can look yourself in the mirror and know you did your best.

CHAPTER 7

JUST A FORM OF TRANSPORT

'You've never lived until you've almost died. For those who fight for it, life has a flavour the protected will never know'

— Guy de Maupassant

There were five things I learned about parachuting in my first two weeks at Brize Norton.

1. Brize Norton is not like Aldershot

We'd been told that, during our fourth month of training, we'd relocate to RAF Brize Norton in Oxfordshire, where we'd learn how to throw ourselves out of a plane and land – hopefully without killing ourselves.

All airborne units go there. If you're in the British Army and you want to learn how to parachute, then you need to put yourself in the hands of the RAF at Brize Norton.

'Like a bloody holiday camp,' Cpl Smith had sniffed at some

stage of the run-up. I, for one, hadn't really understood his full meaning. We were there to learn parachuting, which didn't sound especially relaxing to me.

On arrival, things quickly became clear. Compared to Depot, RAF Brize Norton *is* like a holiday camp. For a start, you're on an RAF base, where the atmosphere is much more relaxed. That means no fitness training or soldiering. Rather, I should say that we were left to keep up our own fitness.

Viciously early mornings? Suddenly a thing of the past. Verbal and physical abuse? Out of the question. Also, we were encouraged rather than ordered. Spoken to, not shouted at.

Our new instructors, who had RAF-sounding titles like 'flight sergeant', wore natty grey jumpsuits and trainers, not boots. They spoke to us like human beings and even occasionally smiled. The reason for the soft touch was soon obvious. What these guys had to say needed to be absorbed and understood by relaxed, receptive and healthy men, not exhausted basket-cases with weakened immune systems.

(Although, just as an aside, it's worth mentioning here that things had changed at Aldershot in that regard. Having passed P Company, our regular instructors had eased off on us a lot. Training was not yet complete, but that phase of it was over, and we felt that bit further along the production line of what we used to call 'the sausage factory'. We were still getting our beastings in the gym, mind you, and still doing the ten-milers. It felt a bit different. A bit more worthy of respect. Put it this way: nobody had called me a northern twat for a while.)

Now, you might wonder, as some of us did, why they kept the parachuting part until last. After all, to go through months of tabbing only to discover that you were petrified of parachuting and couldn't possibly do it wasn't a good use of anyone's time.

Like me, for example. I didn't like heights, never had, and sure enough had been very ginger on the trainasium at Aldershot. 'I'm not sure about jumping out of an aeroplane,' was what I'd said to the careers officer in my old life. He'd smiled and said, 'By the time you come to jump out of one of our aeroplanes, you'll be ready.'

Our instructors would say the same regularly and loudly. 'You have to be tough to throw yourself out of an aircraft,' they'd bawl. 'You have to be fit. The whole point of Para training is to get you ready.'

Ready. That was the key.

Standing in that hangar, I hoped they were right about being ready. And here's a spoiler for you: they were.

2. For our purposes, there are two types of parachuting: static-line and freefall

Later on, I would do plenty of freefall parachuting and we'll get to that in due course. But at Brize Norton, we were being instructed in static-line, where parachutists – all with Bergens attached to their legs – load into an aircraft arranged in what we call sim sticks – or simultaneous sticks – of thirty-two men on one side of the aircraft, thirty-two on the other. You're connected to the line by a D-ring. The aircraft, normally a C-130 Hercules (aka the longest continuously serving military aircraft ever produced), slows down to 120 knots, which is the speed a parachutist can leave an aircraft, the parachutists jump and, as they exit the aircraft, the parachute is deployed. Chances are there'll be dozens of other planes also ditching their sim sticks. A proper *A Bridge Too Far* scene.

The benefit of static-line parachuting is that you get boots on the ground as quickly as possible. Put a bunch of guys on battleships and it can take two or three days to get them to their destination. Paratroopers can board a plane twenty, thirty miles away, even in another country, and be there in the time it takes to fly. Get them out of the plane and on the ground, pick them up two or three days later. Job done.

The drawback, of course, is that a paratrooper is fighting without artillery support or infantry back-up. Everything he does is on his own two feet and carrying his own kit, and that's why it takes a certain type of bloke to be a Para. But that's by-the-by. The careers officer's point stands. Parachuting is a mode of transport. That's all it is.

Freefall is very different. While a static-line parachute is designed to get you from the aeroplane to the ground while carrying a lot of equipment, and is the most efficient way of doing that, a freefall parachute is designed for a jumper with less equipment who needs the benefit of greater manoeuvrability.

A freefall parachutist will exit the aircraft with oxygen at a height of up to 30,000 feet and freefall for two minutes before he or she deploys their own chute. A static-line parachutist, on the other hand, jumps at 800 feet and will be in the air for forty seconds before they hit the ground. And I'm talking about in my day. These days, chutes are designed to open even quicker so paratroopers can jump at even lower altitudes – 600, even 300 feet. Meanwhile, a static-line parachute will generally be round, a freefall parachute square because . . .

3. Square to get you there, round to get you down

Simple as that. The different shapes of the chutes suit different purposes. With the square freefall chute, you can come in very soft, almost landing on tiptoe. But as Paras, we were using bigger military-grade chutes designed to carry 360lbs of weight. That's a paratrooper and their Bergen, as well as mortar tubes, machine-gun re-supplies . . . whatever gear you wanted in your combat zone.

4. You don't pack your own parachute

When you jump in your own time – we call them jollies – is when you pack your own chute. Not in the military. In the military, all the packing is done for you.

5. To pass and receive our wings, we would need to do at least eight jumps

The 'wings', by the way, is the sew-on badge that goes on the upper right arm of your shirt. To earn those wings, we would, over the four weeks of training at Brize Norton, do eight jumps, which would include a balloon jump (we'll get to that), a night jump, a 'clean fatigue' jump (without weapons or equipment) and a 'fatigue jump', which is with full equipment. Everything we did at Brize Norton was leading up to those jumps.

Being an airfield, Brize Norton was vast, much bigger than Aldershot. It's the size of a small town, except a small town with aircraft constantly taking off and landing. In and out all day came the big C-130 Hercules, as well as smaller, lighter aircraft and choppers.

Our home for the duration was hidden away in a corner and consisted of an outside training area and a huge hangar above which was a sign: 'Knowledge Dispels Fear', the motto of the Number One Parachute Training School. One of the first bits of knowledge we acquired was that the RAF don't like marching. When we made our way from the cookhouse to our billets or the PTS hangar, we just . . . walked. We didn't march. Marching was for 'pongos', as the RAF called us, and it got in their way. Fine by us.

At one side of the PTS hangar was a mocked-up C-130 fuselage. In short order, we'd be using it for exit practice. Laid out on the floor were a series of mats below a contraption called the fan, while hanging down were various harnesses.

In fact, these weren't the first bits of training kit we'd seen. Outside in the training area were two Meccano structures: the Tower and the Exit Trainer. They looked like the kind of things you see at fire stations, except much taller – tall enough to put the trainasium to shame. It was on these various bits of kit that we'd learn the art and craft of airborne deployment.

Training began. And it began with a simple question: What is parachuting?

As explained to us by one of the RAF instructors, Capt Rogers – who probably thought he was a strict disciplinarian but was a real pussycat, nothing compared to what we were accustomed to – parachuting boiled down to three things: exit, flight and landing.

Of those three, the very first thing we learned – and the one thing that the RAF instructors would get genuinely angry about if it were neglected – was to always keep your feet and knees together as tight as you possibly can and stick the landing.

You might have a bad exit. You might have a bad flight. But, no matter what, you're going to land, and when you do, you keep your feet and knees together. They drummed this into us again and again. Never land on one leg. Never try to spread the load by leaving your legs wide. Never let any other part of your body take the impact. No, you pull your feet and knees together and then buckle as you make contact, going into a roll so that your whole body hits the ground instead of one part of your body taking all the impact. Rolling onto my back (and, in a real situation, onto my rigging lines) with my legs and knees together may even have been the first thing that I practised.

So, *keep your feet and knees together.* A lot of the big lessons in this book translate well to civvy life. But not that one. That one's just for the parachutists.

Our group had been joined by folk from the All-Arms, one or two of whom I recognized from P Company. We were split into subgroups and taken to get to grips with the various modules. Some of us were learning exit in the Hercules fuselage, some of us going to flight, another group learning landings on the mats.

There was an element new to training, something I hadn't experienced for several months. It was, dare I say it, fun. If you got something wrong, you didn't get screamed at, called a flat-cap wearing thicko and forced to do twenty press-ups. They just made you do it again. After months of gruelling punishment, when everybody had aches and pains from P Company, some of us still limping, it was a blessing. We liked this new Brize Norton. We liked the hours – imagine the joy when we heard that we'd finish at 4.30 p.m. each day – and we really liked the food, which was a cut above Aldershot (sorry Aldershot cookhouse, but it was). And we loved the fact that there were female RAF staff wandering around.

It's fair to say I was enjoying myself by then. I felt like a proper soldier. My fitness was sky-high (we all had what we called the 'screaming skull look', lean and mean) and I was at last being treated like a grown-up. I'd dialled into a disciplined life. I'd learned that the more organized I was, the easier soldiering would be.

And, like everybody else in my platoon, I'd worked out the golden rule: you can enjoy it and you can have fun, but you can never stop paying attention. You never stop learning and you never forget that mistakes have a very high price.

Mistakes or maybe just bad luck. I'll tell you a story. During my years in battalion with Para Reg, I took part in hundreds of drops. Many of them stick in the memory, but this one particularly does because the outcome was so tragic.

We had a full aircraft, which is known as Sim32 – sixty-four men in total, thirty-two each side. The procedure was standard, same as every other. About ten minutes before the jump, instructors come down the two lines of men, checking that each paratrooper's D-ring is secure, his harness properly fixed, equipment safe.

With five minutes to go, each line stands and the men shuffle towards the door, waiting for the moment it opens. Some of the C-130s had big cargo doors at the tail, out of which the parachutists would jump. Ours had doors either side of the main body of the aircraft.

'We're now in position,' they say. 'Two minutes.'

The door opens and whoever is in Position One has the benefit of the safest, least tangle-prone position, albeit with the drawback of having to look out of an open door and into the void for two minutes before the drop.

At the same time, we're all looking at the lights, especially the crew member who has headphones on listening to the pilot saying: 'Stand by, stand by . . .'

Then 'Red on'.

The word goes down the aircraft; everybody knows we're ready to go. That we have about five seconds before . . .

'Green on.'

The light turns green and then 'Go, go, go.'

As all this was happening on your stick, the same is being repeated on the other side. In a perfect world, it would be carefully staggered, but it never really is. The pilot has the aircraft at exactly the right speed in exactly the right place, and you can't hang around. You jump.

I had jumped and, as my canopy dutifully popped, I saw problems not far away.

What had happened was that a lad had come out of the opposite side of the aircraft, another one on my side. They'd collided and become tangled in the air.

This happens. It's much more common than you might think, because even though the two sticks are staggered, it's not an exact science, especially when you're stepping out into a wind of up to 130 knots, with the aircraft itself going at 120 knots. You don't go straight down; you go across into a slipstream and not necessarily in a nice straight line.

What normally transpires when two guys clash is that one of the parachutes becomes dominant. I've seen it on more than one occasion where one canopy has inflated, the other one deflated, two guys have come down on one parachute and been fine. It's a bit hairy and not very nice for all concerned. But it works.

On this occasion, however, the lads weren't so lucky. Heart in mouth, I watched as neither of the canopies inflated. I lost sight of them and as I came earthwards prayed that somehow things had sorted themselves out.

Sadly not. On the ground, I learned that they had come down fast and died of their injuries.

There are, of course, drills in the event of two guys coming out of the aircraft at the same time and finding themselves on a collision course. Firstly, your drill is to shout, 'Steer away, steer away' and then grab one of your rigging lines.

Your rigging lines are what connect your harness to your canopy. You pull on them to spill air from the inflated canopy, which tilts you away from obstacles. It doesn't offer nearly the manoeuvrability of the square chute, but it does give you enough directional control that you can, for example, steer away from a tree or, in this instance, from a fellow parachutist in the sky.

Meanwhile, if collision is inevitable, we're drilled to cross our hands over our equipment in order to minimize the possibility of entanglement. Just as I've seen guys manage to 'steer away' using the first drill, I've seen others bump into each other then come away again, no harm done. Sadly not on this occasion.

Those collision drills were what we practised repeatedly in the PTS hangar at Brize Norton. We also drilled the exit and the landing. And we did it over and over again. The point of the drills was the same as it had been with our weapons drills (and if you're wondering when I'm going to get to weapons, it's not long now) or any other drill. It was so that we would do these things without having to stop and remember them, without having to engage the problem-solving part of our brain which might be employed elsewhere. To make them instinct. Muscle memory.

So we'd clamber aboard that Hercules fuselage on one side of the hangar and jump from it to mats a couple of feet below, and we would do it again and again and again. We'd jump from other structures onto other mats, and we would do it again and again and again. You get the picture.

When we'd done that several thousand times, it was time to move on to the fan, which was a bit of a kit adapted from an old French fairground ride meant to simulate the flight part of the jump followed by the landing. Of course, the landing – the part you had to get right. Those legs had to be together. You had to roll properly. I'd thought that learning to land and roll would be as easy as . . . well, as easy as falling off a log. But it wasn't so. At first, it took concentration to remember where my legs should go and how to keep my arms out of the way. But then, through repetition, it became second nature.

We practised other things as well, including canopy handling and a technique called 'harness release and drag', which was the procedure if your parachute inflated while on the ground. This involved getting out of the harness and collecting the parachute by picking one set of webbing lines and pulling on it to deflate the chute while at the same time preventing the parachute from pulling you along the ground.

And flight? For that, they clipped us into training harnesses that hung from the roof. This involved learning the safety count, which went 'One thousand, two thousand, three thousand, check canopy' and look.

By the time you look, your parachute, activated by the static-line of the aircraft, should have deployed. As the bloke hanging underneath it, it's your job to check that, firstly, it has deployed correctly and, secondly and thirdly, it has no holes, a good shape, and so on and so forth.

This whole time, your hands are on the release for your reserve chute, and if the sight-check of the main chute wasn't satisfactory, then out came the reserve. Assuming this wasn't necessary, next you'd concentrate on making sure there was no other parachutist in the vicinity. If there was, then you went to one of the drills I've previously described.

By the time of the second week, we were feeling well drilled and ready for the bits of kit outside the tower and the exit trainer – bigger, taller versions of what we had learned inside, which, of course, would build us up to the first real test: the balloon jump.

THE TAKEAWAY

There are only two fears. 'Am I good enough?' and 'What if I fail?'

Now, when we're confronted with a situation that's outside our comfort zone, our minds go to three places: the past, the present and the future. We look over the past, full of regret, thinking about what we should have done differently, re-living times when we were unpleasant to people or they were unpleasant to us. This affects our experience of the present, which is where we should be, living in the moment, and it feeds into the future, where we imagine worst-case scenarios, again affecting our behaviour in the present.

Now, if that effect is beneficial, great. If it means you spend extra time checking your rigging, then all power to it. But what if it prevents you from living your life? Then you need to do something about it; you need to remember that if you can conjure a future in which you fail, then you can do the same for a future in which you succeed.

'Easier said than done, Des,' you sigh.

I hear you. Maybe you won't manage it. But just being aware of it helps. It allows you to see those thoughts for what they are: carriers of those two fears: 'Am I good enough?' and 'What if I fail?'

CHAPTER 8

KAMIKAZE DES, PART ONE

'All men dream; but not equally. Those who dream by night in the dusty recesses of their minds awake to find that it was vanity, but the dreamers of the day are dangerous men. That they may act their dreams with open eyes to make it possible . . .'

– T.E. Lawrence

Following SAS selection, I returned to Brize Norton, this time for training in stealth jumps, which can and do happen in utmost secrecy. Small groups of operators, fours or eights, working on clandestine operations and usually behind enemy lines, will deploy from a cargo plane whose appearance on a radar can easily be explained. They jump from a great height using oxygen, which is required for jumps over a certain height.

I took part in hundreds of such jumps, both in training and on active service, freefalling for more than two minutes and reaching speeds of more than 120 miles an hour, which in parachuting terms is terminal velocity – the maximum speed a human being can reach falling through the air. (In actual fact, I can exceed terminal velocity by changing the shape of my body while in the air, but that's a conversation for another day.)

The idea is that enemy ground troops cannot detect an insertion this way. They don't see or hear the aircraft from which you have jumped, will often disregard a radar blip as being a non-military aircraft and they certainly don't register the parachutist. A parachutist can exit his aircraft and land two minutes later, and do so in a completely silent fashion.

And that's the whole idea of freefall. The principles are similar to static-line parachuting with some key differences, one of them being the fact that you tend not to be laden down with lots of gear – although you will, of course, have your weapons and webbing, and you'll be dealing with oxygen.

Problems in freefalling tend to occur in one of two ways. First, there might be an oxygen malfunction, a situation in which you risk getting hypoxaemia. One of our training exercises involved being cooped up in a vacuum container from which they would extract oxygen. When we were asked to do mathematical equations, we couldn't. You can't do simple adding and multiplying. You stop being able to think straight, and that obviously is a huge fear.

The second-most common issue is with the opening of the chute, and that's when my own issues cropped up.

It was during freefall training that my eventual nickname began to take root. That nickname was 'Kamikaze Des', which, of course, is a bit misleading because it was not as though I was deliberately throwing myself into dangerous situations; they were being forced upon me. But I was the malfunction king.

There were three incidents that earned me my nickname. I

lived to tell the tale and the reason for that is because I didn't panic. We have a saying in the military, when panic takes hold in a moment of crisis or danger: your mind 'blows up'. The reason that my mind never blew up in any of those three incidents was training and drills. It's a philosophy that works in the military; I firmly believe it can work in real life too, and I'll explain why in a bit.

But first, my Kamikaze Des stories – and an introduction to the reserve drill.

When you have a bad chute, the drill is to cut free the malfunctioning canopy and then go to the reserve. It's called 'cutting away, even though no cutting is involved. On your harness is a pad and handle. You peel and punch to get rid of the main chute and then pull for the reserve. If you put a fresh chute on top of a bad chute, the chances are it is going to tangle up, so you must get rid of the bad chute first.

This is a different drill from the static-line parachuting procedure where you don't cut away your main chute; you just deploy the reserve. The reasons for this are that, firstly, you're only at 800 feet and you don't have time. Secondly, it's very, very rare for a static-line parachute not to deploy and, as a result, harnesses don't have the functionality of freefall. You can't cut away.

Is that a good policy? Probably. I've never seen an incident where a static-line parachute hasn't deployed properly (apart from in a collision), so the thinking is sound. However, what I have seen is when a guy has panicked that his main chute hasn't deployed then opened the reserve, only for the two chutes to fight each other. In many of those instances, one of the chutes will fall away and the other inflate. I've seen it happen where both chutes have opened together and the parachutist has come down on two chutes. And I've also seen where the two were fighting together, neither inflating properly, and the parachutist has come down dangerously fast but thankfully come to no harm.

So that's the drill as it applies to reserves. I should also add that, in freefalling, we often have what's called an AOD – or automatic opening device – attached with wires and triggered by barometer pressure. I'm not a fan of the AOD; not many are. The reason why is that you've just jumped from a great height, wanting the AOD to kick in at pulling height, which in military terms is 3,000 feet. This means you've dropped a long way and reached terminal velocity. In this kind of environment, the AOD won't always work. We have altimeters on our wrists – basically big clocks telling you your altitude – and if your chute hasn't automatically deployed by 3,000 feet, then you need to go into manual override sharpish. That in itself can be a little bit dicey, given that you're usually jumping at night, your goggles are misted up and the wrist altimeter may have misted up as well.

These are all reasons why freefall parachuting at night is a dangerous business. You need to have your wits about you and you need to be able to think fast and react faster.

So, anyway, back to the story ... I was jumping with an instructor and doing so without the aid of an AOD in order to get the hang of manually deploying the chute at 3,000 feet.

Before the jump, which was from the tailgate of the aircraft, I was briefed. The instructor told me what he was looking for was a good clean exit and control. 'Des, I want to see control. I want to see you do a move left, then a move right. I want to see you come in, just touch me but in a good stable position. And when I wave you off, I want you to turn away, get your own space and then, at 3,000 feet, deploy. Are we clear?'

Yup. Thumbs-up.

We jumped, did the exercise and the instructor pulled away. No need to worry about him. My altimeter told me it was time to pull, so I pulled.

'One thousand, two thousand, three thousand, check.'

I looked up.

Some parachutes pop right away with a crack like snapping a towel in the school changing rooms.

Others take their sweet time. You'll have a squeaky-bum second or so where you wonder if it's going to open as it rolls, leisurely unfurls and then pops.

Either way, you get the pop. The pop is what you're after.

But, this time, there was nothing of the sort. And, looking up, I saw what we call 'a bundle of washing', a weak chute trying to sort itself out.

'Four thousand, five thousand . . .'

It's only you who can decide what to do with a bad chute. But you need to do *something* because the closer you get to the ground, the less chance you have of being able to act. Time is what you're short of, but time is what you need because you must allow for the seconds it takes to cut away the first chute, deploy your reserve and still land safely. When you're screaming towards the ground at 120 miles an hour, it takes about nineteen seconds to cover 1,000 feet. At those speeds, if you deploy, check and then cut, you have about fifteen seconds to get a canopy above your head before it's ineffective.

So I had to make a decision.

Quick.

There was a conversation I'd had with the instructor a few days before, the same instructor with whom I'd jumped, who'd peeled away and who, if he was looking, was probably wondering what the hell was going on with me. We'd been talking about the chute deployment protocol specifically as it applied to the reserve.

I'd said, 'I hear guys saying you should take your time, have faith in the main chute. Is that right?'

The point was that main chutes so rarely failed. They might not always pop as quickly as you'd like, but they'd get there in the end.

'Des,' he said to me, 'I've done thousands on thousands of freefalls and, let me tell you, there is only one drill, only one, and it's this: if you don't like what you see above your head, get rid of it. You have a reserve parachute. That reserve will always open. So when your mind blows up and you're stressed, just remember that one drill: if you don't like the chute above your head, cut it away, get on the reserve. That's it.'

Which is all very well. But . . .

It's bloody terrifying having to deploy your reserve. You must get rid of your main, cut it away. You have to deploy the reserve, a process that involves peeling away a Velcro flap and then punching the release, and there's a chance that if the drill doesn't go well, the two might become tangled up. There's the psychological aspect of knowing you've just had a final roll of the dice, that you've used your insurance policy, and if the reserve doesn't work, you're toast. It's the only thing stopping you from ending your parachuting career and, indeed, your entire life as an impact stain on the ground below.

So that's why parachutists give the first chute time to do its thing. You're willing that first chute to pop. You're desperate for it to inflate. What if you end up cutting away a perfectly good chute? And it's all very well for the instructor to say, 'The reserve will always open', but maybe this is the one time it doesn't. After all, I've had one failure.

But no. You can't dither. You can't cross your fingers and hope. You must make a decision. And you have to make it fast.

I went to the drill. Peel, punch, *boom*. Away went the first chute. 'One thousand, two thousand, three thousand, check.' My reserve popped. It is, by the way, of equal quality to the main. It's not like the spare tyre on your car. It's the same size and shape and build with the same line and toggles – toggles that I used to spill air from the underside of the canopy and land safely.

I like to tell stories, I cannot lie. And one of the most common questions I'm asked about this one is: Was there a problem with the parachute? Was it faulty?

One answer is that you can rarely say either way. Another answer is that it probably wasn't faulty at all. It was just . . . slow. Probably if I'd given it another ten seconds (which no way was I going to do), it might have opened. But this is exactly what I'm saying about the drill; it didn't matter if it was a bad chute or not. What mattered was that I decided it was. And I went to the drill.

The other question is: 'How do you stop yourself from panicking?' The answer again goes to the drills. It's the same reason you don't panic when somebody opens fire on you, or when the guy next to you is hit, or when something explodes nearby. It's a drill. It's automatic action; when your mind blows up and, in your highly adrenalized state, you can't think straight, you just go into that instinctive action.

I make no excuses about droning on about drills. The fact is that everybody in the military loves them – because they work. Like I say, it's a principle I believe extends to civvy life. *If you want to do something well, you practise it.* An actor acquaintance of mine told me that his performance improves tenfold when he knows the lines so well he no longer has to think about them. The bit of his brain engaged in listening for his cue and making sure he's got the next line right is instead focused on his performance. That's why they call it being well-drilled. Practice. Whether it's a wedding speech or parallel parking in that tight spot outside your house, *practise. Make it instinctive. Go to your drill.*

Another important thing regarding drills is that you keep them simple. Basic planning and straight basic drills will win the day every day. Everything is kept very simple. You see the guards on parade. They call that drill too. For a lot of men to do the same thing all at once, there's a complexity there, so they drill it repeatedly and become very good at it. You'll notice that the words of command are very simple. If there are too many words of command, people are going to be wondering, *What did he say?*

Anyway, back on the ground, my instructor and I talked through what had happened. I mainly wanted to know whether I'd done something wrong.

'No, Des, you did the right drill. It's only you who can make that decision, and the decision you made was correct. You know why? Because you're standing here now.'

Those words from the instructor lead me on to another incident, another reason why I ended up with my Kamikaze Des nickname.

THE TAKEAWAY

So much of what I was doing back then was about conquering fear, so you'll forgive me if I add to what I've already said on the matter. The fact is, I've got plenty to say on the subject because I've gained a lot of knowledge over the years. And, as the saying goes, knowledge dispels fear.

Nowhere was that principle illustrated better than in learning how to throw yourself out of an aeroplane. Your fear asks you, 'What if the chute doesn't open?' Your knowledgeable brain reminds you that the chute literally has one job and that job is to open. It is designed to unfurl. It wants to open. It goes back to what I was saying about trusting in the systems. But you can only do that when you understand the system.

My advice, then, is just this: to take the first steps towards overcoming your fear, start by learning more about it, understanding how it ticks.

This applies to parachuting, of course, but it can also apply elsewhere. Say you've got to do a speech at a wedding. Go to the venue early and get a feel for the room. You'll be practising your speech over and over – and if not, why not? – so why not try it out in the venue ahead of time? Call it prep. Call it research or study. But everything you do to familiarize yourself with that big monolithic fear will chip away at it, making things easier for you in the long run.

CHAPTER 9

KAMIKAZE DES, PARTS TWO AND THREE

'Chasing angels or fleeing demons, go to the mountains'
– Jeffrey Rasley

I was with the Regiment, training in Scandinavia. I wasn't there to learn about parachuting, but found myself involved anyway. This was a region characterized by its mountainous terrain, with teams skilled at flying between peaks and using the square-canopied chutes to land with pinpoint accuracy in tricky places.

Another thing specific to the area is a love of hot-air ballooning. You'd look up and see, say, a tractor hanging from one. And this being Scandinavia, the occupants of the tractor would be waving at you. They're nice people, the Scandinavians.

It came to my last day there and, having expressed an interest in the balloons, it was suggested that I jump from one, something I hadn't done since Basic with the Paras. The day came, though, and sadly the weather just wasn't right for balloon jumping. Such a shame. I would have loved to have jumped out of a tractor.

Instead, they took me up in a light aircraft ideally suited to the mountainous terrain – one that could land on a dime and loved to negotiate the peaks. So the question shifted to: 'Des, would you like to jump out of this light aircraft onto a mountain?'

'Sure,' I said. 'Sounds great.' I got togged up and off we went, first to one mountain, where I took a bunch of pictures, and then off to another, about twenty minutes' flight away. The mountains were stunning and I remember thinking, *That's the army for you. The adverts don't lie. You end up going to places you only ever saw in films as a kid.*

'Do you like the view?' my principal guide Christophe asked me. He was the kind of guy who always had a half-smile playing on his lips and a mischievous look in his eyes. There was also nothing he didn't know about parachuting and the mountains. I'd liked him from the moment I met him. He always called me Desmond even though my name is Derek, and he was such a nice bloke that I didn't have the heart to correct him.

'Love it,' I told them.

'Well, today it is your lucky day then, Desmond, because you're going to jump.'

What? *Now?*

They're funny guys, the Scandies. Before you know it, they had the door open and were going, 'Off you go, Des. Three, two, one . . . Go.'

But I'd done hundreds of jumps by then, static-line and free-fall, and I wasn't fazed. It was, after all, my job not to be fazed.

I jumped.

'One thousand, two thousand, three thousand, check.'

I looked up and it wasn't right.

Oops, I thought, checking my altimeter.

Twelve thousand feet. Plenty of time yet.

Right?

A couple of hours later, I was sitting with Christophe in a café at the foot of the mountain and we were discussing the jump, specifically the malfunction. Christophe was not the type to get cross. But he wasn't very happy with me. I'll tell you why.

When I'd looked up, what I saw was that the chute had deployed but was not behaving properly, by which I mean there was no pop. No complete inflation. It seemed to me that it was twisting of its own accord.

Watching from the plane, Christophe had spotted that I had a 'line over' situation where one of the canopy lines has found its way over the top of the chute and is preventing full inflation. He'd said to himself, 'Cut away, Desmond. Cut away now.'

That's easy to say when you're in the plane. Me, I had 12,000 feet on the altimeter. And as I've already explained, no parachutist wants to cut away and go to their reserve, not if they can help it. As I've also said, canopies have a way of sorting themselves out. The job of a canopy is to inflate and a canopy wants to do its job.

This chute didn't sort itself out, though. When I checked my altimeter again, I was at 7,000 feet. Of course, by now the thought of having to cut away had occurred to me, but at the same time, I was thinking, *It'll sort itself out in a bit.* Don't forget, I had a lot of experience under my belt at this stage.

But crucially, not experience of mountain parachuting.

And that's why Christophe's usual twinkliness had been replaced by something else as we sat at the café.

'You had a malfunction, Desmond,' he said darkly. 'I saw you look and establish that your chute had not inflated.'

'It was partially open, though.'

This was true. The chute, while not working properly, was halfway to doing its job. It was just ... not quite there. And I knew I was falling too fast. Leg-breakingly, spine-snappingly too fast. At 6,000 feet, I decided to cut.

So I cut it away. Peel and punch and so on. The second chute popped – *shoom* – doing exactly what it was supposed to do. And now I was on a safe canopy, steering my way towards the drop zone. I landed perfectly okay and gathered my parachute up. My heart was beating fast; there was no doubt about it. But, again, I had gone to my drill.

'You waited too long to get rid of your canopy.'

'I established an issue at twelve. Around seven, I went to the reserve. I didn't think that I was cutting it especially fine.'

He shook his head and, pointing at the mountain, said, 'That mountain is more than 12,000 feet to the ground, from the tip to the base, but not all of it is to the ground. You see the shape of it? It's like a Christmas tree. You were very close to hitting one of the peaks. Very close.'

'Was I?'

'I was watching you, Desmond. You were. Next time you have a problem, you cut away. You get on the reserve canopy quick. If you don't like what you see, get rid of the parachute.'

It's an interesting case. I'm a great believer in listening to instinct and I was trained to go to the reserve drill if I didn't like what I was seeing with the main. And, no doubt about it, I didn't like what I was seeing. At the same time, I was hoping it would sort itself out. It was a good day. There was nice light. I had sufficient height.

But I didn't take the environment into account. And I didn't go to my drill quickly enough.

This is another aspect of drills. There's no point in having a drill if you're not going to go to it. A drill isn't a last resort. It isn't an admission of failure. It's just another thing to try.

Of course, word got back to my buddies in the Regiment. Another chute failure.

Even then, I'm not sure when the 'Kamikaze Des' nickname was minted. I think that might have come after a training exercise in Africa where we jumped out the back of an aircraft and deployed right away in order to work on our canopy skills, navigation and so forth.

On this particular occasion, out we came, four of us almost at the same time. I deployed, but could almost hear my mate shouting at me – 'Des, bad canopy, get rid of it' – or words to that effect.

Sure enough, the chute was flapping. Not inflating properly, not popping. And so, without further ado, I cut it away and went to the reserve.

Textbook. It only took three failures, but I got it. When the chute's not doing what it's supposed to do, you go to the reserve.

No doubt it was after that that I got the nickname because to have three chute failures is quite a rarity.

Even so, that last one was probably the least risky, simply for timing reasons. It's all about how low you are when you deploy your chute. I've seen guys come down to 1,000 feet before deploying and they've been banned. In military parachuting, they like you to pull at 3,500 feet; in civvy parachuting, 2,500 feet. The reason for this is that civvy parachutes are much more manoeuvrable and react quicker than military chutes, which are a bit bigger and a bit more cumbersome.

Each of my three malfunctions could well have been fatal had I not had time to sort them out. This is why I say make your decision early. (It's vital in parachuting, but it applies to 'normal' life too, I think.) Problems will eat away at height, and height is time. Remember, if you pull at 3,500 feet, you're not really under the canopy until around 3,000 feet. I've known guys who played with the main chute, then been too late to deploy the reserve, hit the ground and died. I've known guys who have deployed their reserve too late and ended up breaking their legs.

I saw a video of a guy once who was having real problems. His parachute was flapping and even though his fellow jumpers were shouting at him, he didn't seem to be doing anything about it. Now, you never know what's happening in the sky. His arm might have got trapped or even broken, or he might have got it stuck in the rigging lines. Whatever it was, it took him an age to get it sorted. He was maybe only 300 feet off the ground when his canopy went pop.

At 300 feet, it's very, very tight. The chances are that he'll have hurt himself on landing simply because the chute hadn't had a chance to do its job properly. But he didn't die. That's the important thing. He didn't end up as a stain on the grass. What we're saying here is that the drills we have are there for a reason. They're there to save your life and if you abuse them, there's a very good chance that you might not live to tell the tale. Parachuting is a dangerous business. That's why we have the drills to deal with it.

THE TAKEAWAY

Drills. Can't talk about them enough. The word 'drill' indicates that something is done automatically, whether it's a weapons drill, a parachute drill, a march or whatever. The action is drilled into you. We have a saying in the military: 'Train hard, fight easy'. Just as it sounds, it's a motto that means the more you do in training, planning and preparation, the more efficient you'll be when you come to do it for real.

When we're training, we're generally practising contact with the enemy. Actually fighting the enemy is a scary thing to do. When it gets loud, your mind blows and that's when you need your drills – in other words, that's when you need well-practised, automatic reactions. The more you practise, the more you train, the more efficient you become. We practise as much as we can to simulate the real scenario so that when you're exposed to the real thing, you're more likely to have a successful outcome.

Even today, outside of the military, I find myself going into drills. I still have that mindset because you can put drills to anything. I know that I work better in the morning, so I get up early, start work, and that's a drill. Anything you do automatically is a drill, and when you drill it, it becomes automatic.

CHAPTER 10

JUMP NUMBER ONE

'The future belongs to those who believe in the beauty
of their dreams'

– Eleanor Roosevelt

Back to Brize Norton, and the next thing you know, we had a
week of theory in the can and were outside, gazing up at a huge
hot-air balloon tethered to a winch mounted on a Bedford. Not
an *Around the World in 80 Days*-style balloon – more a barrage-
type balloon in keeping with the military setting.

Six of us, plus an instructor, boarded the basket. With the
winch whirring, the balloon was raised to 800 feet. Throughout
my childhood, I'd been scared of heights. I remembered what I'd
said to the careers officer, telling him about my fear. I remembered his reply. *You'll be ready.*

Was I, though?

I was. Just about.

Now, the thing about the balloon is that it's not the 'soft'
entry into parachuting you might imagine. In an aircraft, you're

attached to a line, on top of which you're a Para, so you do what your commanding officer tells you to do, which is follow the man in front in order that you don't hold up the guy behind. There's something about the noise and urgency and imperative of jumping out of an aircraft that makes it easier. The aircrew are shouting at you to go. The instructors are bundling you out. The guy ahead has just jumped. Of course you're going to go. It's almost a relief when you jump.

Not in a balloon. It's quieter than an aircraft, obviously. Almost eerily quiet. Added to this, you can see everything as you leave the comfort of the ground. You have plenty of time to contemplate launching yourself into space.

For these reasons, a lot of guys will bottle it the first time. Guys who'll go on to jump out of aircraft will take more persuading to step out of the cage. You have a line. It deploys your chute. Otherwise? Different ballgame.

'Step forward,' said the instructor, raising the bar. 'Go when you like.'

Shit. I'd been hoping for 'Three, two, one . . .' and all that malarkey. But no. We'd been warned that if something went wrong with the cable or winch and the balloon came adrift – as does sometimes happen – then the instructor would deploy us as quickly as possible. I found myself half-wishing that would happen just to give the jump a bit of imperative and some urgency. I wanted the impulse to go taken out of my hands.

And, of course, it's all being done on purpose. You guessed it: the balloon jump is a bottle test. It's simply to establish whether you have the guts to step forward and take that little jump – because you must step away from the cage for fear of hitting the parachute on the cage – and go straight down. Everything else was taken care of for me. I was on a static-line on the balloon. It was just about overcoming my fear of heights. Even now, my palms are sweating just thinking about it.

They really are. That's how I get when I talk about parachuting. I remember looking down, thinking that you could forget the high dive at the swimming pool – *this* was a jump. And I remember having to step out but taking a proper step so that the chute didn't catch the back of the cage.

'Hands across.'

That's the next command. You have to put your hands across your reserve parachute. One thing we'd been told was that if the main chute didn't work, then you had to get on to your reserve much more quickly than in a normal jump, chiefly because of the height. When I thought about it, that seemed to translate as: *You need to think quicker on this jump, your first jump, than on any other subsequent jump*, which obviously slightly blew my mind.

So I stepped forward.

The bar was raised.

And I stepped out.

Eight hundred feet is not high, not for parachuting purposes. The chute came out almost immediately, unfurling behind me like wings opening, and I glided gently to the ground, going to my landing drill, which of course felt like second nature.

Since learning parachuting, I've taken part in hundreds and hundreds of jumps. I've done it as part of active service, but I also do it for sport. No doubt about it, though: that balloon jump was the hardest. But I got through it – and all the subsequent jumps – to earn my wings.

It was at the end of our month in Brize Norton that we were given the wings and had them stitched onto our shirts. At the same time, we were awarded our berets, the disastrous 'pork pie' beret that we quickly stashed in favour of better ones that we bought from the famous Victor's, in Aldershot.

Now we were paratroopers, expected to wear our wings and our maroon beret while on camp as we worked out the final fortnight or so of our training. There was a lot of marching in that period, I remember, but we didn't care. We had a pass-out parade complete with awards for champion recruit, champion SLR shot and champion GPMG shot (aka general-purpose machine-gun shot). My parents were there to watch me pass out and saw me awarded with my trophy for best GPMG shot.

After that, we were given a couple of weeks before joining Battalion. I chose 1 Para because I heard it was more fitness-minded, which interested me. And that was where I went. Not that I 'went' anywhere, as 1 Para was based in Aldershot. And that was it. That was where I'd be for the next eight years.

But there's a nice little postscript to the tale of my Para training, which isn't just a story of me learning how to be a soldier but me learning how to be a man. Just as I had finished training during that period before the pass-out parade, I was on my way to the cookhouse one day when I spotted a guy striding towards me. *He looks familiar,* I thought, but I couldn't place him. Yet he was approaching me with one hand outstretched, saying, 'Hello, Des? Do you remember me?'

It hit me. Of course, I knew him. Of course, I did. It was the careers officer.

We shook hands warmly. I don't mind saying he was fair glowing with pride.

'Congratulations, Des,' he said. 'I knew you'd make it.'

THE TAKEAWAY

'Feel the fear but do it anyway' is a motto I live by. Doing that balloon jump – a bottle jump, remember – I realized that from that point on I'd be doing a lot of scary shit. And it struck me that there are times in life when you've just got to do what you've got to do, no matter how hard or scary. You must meet your fear head on. Feel it but do it anyway.

Most stress is believed to be caused by inaction. It's not doing the job; it's making a decision about doing the job that is stressing you.

In other words, you're procrastinating. Maybe you're dithering over a house move. Make a decision. 'No, we'll stay here for another couple of years.' It's making the decision that removes the stress. 'I need to sort the car out, but I'm putting it off.' Get it booked in. You'll feel the stress fall away. Take action. It need not be something drastic. Just decide.

CHAPTER 11

THE MINDSET

'Fear is a state of mind, created by an illusionist, a trickster of emotion that devalues our perception of an event, manipulating our reaction, and constructs a version of reality that statistically, will never happen'

– Anon

I mentioned how training at Depot had introduced me to the idea of using my initiative to follow orders. At the same time, it had indoctrinated me in what I call the Para mindset. It would be remiss of me not to tell a couple of tales from my days with 1 Para that illustrate one or both at work.

After several years in Battalion, and having been promoted to lance-corporal, I was leading a small team working the Sham Chun River, which acts as a natural border between Hong Kong, which was UK-controlled at the time, and mainland China, where our opposite number was the People's Liberation Army or the PLA.

Being a narrow waterway close to Kowloon, Sham Chun was

used by IIs – illegal immigrants – who could then move on to Kowloon. Our job was to stop them from doing that.

Even though the river was only 30 feet wide, no IIs tried the crossing during the day. Too risky. At night, we'd sit with a flask of tea, have our sandwiches, keep dead quiet, watch out for torchlight and then pick up the IIs as they arrived. Either that or we'd wait until daybreak and scour the shore to find immigrants huddled in hidey-holes, presumably hoping to out-wait us. Any we found would be given a cup of tea, put into a Land Rover and sent back over the bridge with a regretful wave. Poor sods.

It's fair to say that our approach was different to that of the PLA on the other side, who wanted to stop them from making the journey in the first place . . .

Put it this way: we began finding bodies in the river. About once a week, this was. At first, we were like, *Well, maybe they drowned.* But then we started seeing signs of beatings. The PLA – because who else would it be? – were either getting careless or wanted to send a message. As you can imagine, it was pretty grim making these discoveries. I mean, it wasn't the nicest job in the first place, having to capture people – who, after all, were just hoping for a better life – and send them back to an uncertain future. Having to fish out bodies from the river was another matter entirely, and we thought, *Hang on, what are we doing here? Are we sending these people back so they can return to their villages? Or are we sending them back so they can catch a beating, maybe even be killed for their troubles?*

So, I decided (initiative alert) that no way was I sending them back. Returning IIs so that the PLA could beat them to a pulp? Or beat them to death? No way.

Exercise in Wales (Para Regt)

Patrolling (Para Regt)

Martial arts
training
(Para Regt)

Physical
training and
flexing (SAS)

Physical training instructor (Para Regt)

One arm press-ups (Para Regt)

439 Platoon Aldershot 1977 (Para Regt)

Freefall parachuting, Europe (SAS)

On oxygen, 25,000 ft, ready to jump (SAS)

Sky diving with the boys (SAS)

Picked up by boat after parachuting into the sea (SAS)

Exercise in
Africa (SAS)

Training black
kit (SAS)

Mobility training in Africa (SAS)

Always time for tea and biscuits (SAS)

We used to patrol with an interpreter and, from that moment on, me and my team, instead of doing what we'd normally do with an II – tea, Land Rover, regretful wave etc. – we'd do the tea bit, maybe even a sandwich if we had any spare, and then let them go.

I remember the first time it happened. In the party was an old lady, maybe the grandmother. To think of sending them back to maybe find their way beneath the rifle butts of the PLA was . . .

No. Just no.

I pointed to where we could see the lights twinkling in the distance. 'Hong Kong?' I said. 'Hong Kong?'

Heartbreakingly, they thought I was taunting them until, at last, the penny dropped, with the help of the interpreter. They thanked me and left to continue their journey.

I remember one night that we caught a man and a woman. I handed my flask of tea over and the guy, presumably parched, grabbed it and took a huge slug of scalding hot tea. Next thing you know, he was in a right state and we were having to calm him down with cool liquids before making his day by sending him on his way.

Things got particularly hairy on one evening. We became aware of a commotion on the opposite bank. As I say, the river was only 20–30 metres wide, so whatever was happening wasn't far away. Screaming, shouting. Torchlight bouncing up and down in the trees and undergrowth.

Now I could make out figures. PLA soldiers roughing up somebody who was on the ground. You didn't need to be Sherlock Holmes to know what was going on.

We were equipped with ultra-powerful Dragon torches. You

activated one of those and, *shoom*, the whole place was lit up like daytime in the Gobi Desert. Super bright.

And that was it. Our presence announced, the beating stopped. The soldiers looked over, looked across the bank, across the river access, shielding their eyes, reaching for their weapons.

'Tell them to stop,' I told the interpreter and did something that in retrospect I shouldn't have done. I cocked my SLR.

It was just a gesture but, with the benefit of hindsight, I realize it was overly warlike, and it was no surprise when they reached for their own weapons, which hung on slings.

In response, I put the SLR to my shoulder. My men did the same. To the interpreter, I said, 'Tell them to stop that. Tell them that we know that bodies we've been finding in the river are down to them. Tell them this is not our job. This is not what we do.'

The interpreter was trying to be diplomatic, claiming that the guys weren't responsible for the bodies.

'Either way,' I said, 'we can see what they're up to right now. Tell them to stop.'

Talk about fake it until you make it. I'll be honest with you; I was shitting it. This was not good. If shots were fired, we were talking about a major, major diplomatic incident.

At the same time, that bloody-minded Para mindset had kicked in. Para mindset plus Des Powell's idea of initiative equals a combustible combination. Fortunately, they saw sense. The moment passed and the guy was let go.

I relaxed. My men relaxed. I knew that, in any firefight, we would have prevailed because that's the way it was. We had that mentality. That Para mindset I keep talking about. You can face up to us, but you're going to come off second best. It's not exactly the prettiest, most subtle philosophy, and it prompted a kind of siege mentality that didn't always produce the most desirable results – possibly not those the British Army would have preferred anyway.

For example, every three weeks or so, we'd go to Hong Kong or Kowloon and let off steam. Bearing in mind that we were out almost every night patrolling the river, fighting insects and humidity and the cramped unpleasant conditions of our billets, you can appreciate that there was plenty of steam to let off.

A favourite hangout for 1 Para was a place called the China Fleet Club, which was also the favourite hangout of American and Australian sailors. We'd get drinking with them and relations were pretty good. These guys would have to watch out for their shore patrol military policemen, who wore white and carried big black batons. The penalty for drunkenness was a night in the brig.

So, anyway, one night we were there with some of these guys having a drink and they were checking their watches, worried about the arrival of the shore patrol. Sure enough, a little jeep full of these white-clad guys turns up. They gestured at our new friends to get back to the ship. Curfew was over. Whatever. But being Paras, we were having none of it.

'Tell them to fuck off,' I said, really winding these guys up.

It worked. In short order, our new drinking buddies were winding up the MPs, whose faces were getting redder in response. This was a night that had included dancing on the bar and lots of friendly banter between the Paras, the Aussies and the Americans, only to spill outside into the street, so it wasn't as if they needed a great deal of winding up.

We were up on the steps of the China Fleet Club, giving it all that at the shore patrol, who had taken up their batons and were doing the classic thing, slapping them against their open palms. Nightsticks or not, they were well outnumbered and knew it, so they soon beat a retreat.

Overjoyed with our victory, we went on a tour of our other favourite Hong Kong drinking holes, moving from the China Fleet Club to an Aussie bar called the Waltzing Matilda and another one called the Bottoms-Up Club. One of the American lads was armed with a camera and took loads of pictures. We ended up staying in touch and him sending me the evidence.

Was it also that night that I invented the squaddie sport of taxi surfing? For the purposes of the story, let's say it was. Me and some lads were in one of the distinctive yellow taxis with red roofs that they had in the city while another load of squaddies were in a second taxi. We were all egging our respective drivers to drive faster and faster, until yours truly decided that things would be a lot tastier if he climbed onto the roof and hung on – literally 'surfing' the taxi.

Even though when the taxi stopped, I slid down the windscreen and off the bonnet to land in a heap on the floor, the whole sketch caught on and pretty soon we were taxi surfing from the China Fleet to the Bottoms-Up every time we were in town.

However, our patronage of the China Fleet Club didn't last long. The club had rooms upstairs where you could go to sleep off a heavy session. Me and a mate went there one night and ended up walking along the ledges that ran on the outside of the building, the mixture of alcohol and Para rendering us completely bombproof. Or so we thought.

It might have been that that got us banned from the China Fleet Club. Or maybe it was the fact that there was a huge fight between rival British squaddies. Although a bunch of other units were involved, it was 1 Para who got the bad name, probably deservedly so. The British MPs could pick us out of a crowd. Cropped hair, desert boots, jeans and sweatshirt – we all wore the same. They'd approach us at the beginning of a night, warning us not to get into any trouble. These warnings sadly tended to fall on deaf ears.

But that's the Paras for you. I'll tell you another story. Often on a weekend, I'd pop over to Milton Keynes, partly to see my mum, who lived there, and partly to hang out with mates.

I'd go out wearing civvy clothes, of course, but I probably looked a bit Para with the cropped hair, sweatshirt, etc. There were some lads in one of the pubs who must have taken a dislike to me, an antipathy that had clearly been growing over several visits, because one night I was in the pub and one of my mates said to me, 'Des, be careful of those lads over there. Apparently, they don't like you.'

There were three of them. One of them in particular, let's call him Punchy, was really eyeballing me.

I was like, *What? How on earth did that happen?* I didn't know these guys from Adam. What's more, I only visited Milton Keynes once in a blue moon and there were hardly Hong Kong levels of hellraising going on – just a few quiet pints in the pub. God knows where their dislike had come from. Still, that's just the way it goes sometimes, I guess.

So, anyway, one of my friends back in Para Reg had bought himself a new Golf GTI and I invited him to come down to Milton

Keynes with me. 'Come on, it'll be a good laugh, you can meet my mates' – that kind of sketch. We were based in Edinburgh at the time and so he said, 'Okay, I'll take the new motor, give it a bit of a run.' Another lad decided to join us and we had ourselves a Para party. We all piled into the car, went to Milton Keynes, did a bit of shopping and in the evening visited a pub.

Who should be in there? Punchy and his mates. So what? We were up for a bit of a laugh, chatting away to some girls, nothing too rowdy. Just enjoying ourselves.

Come closing time, we left the pub and wouldn't you know it, at the same time, so did Punchy and co. As if by magic, they appeared, jostling me in the doorway. The next thing you know, me and Punchy were trading blows right outside the pub.

To his credit, he stood his ground, and I stood mine. For a moment or so, it was a fair fight until one of his mates jumped on my back, a human rucksack for a second, until one of my pals threw a punch and there was a brief scuffle on the sidelines. That fight fizzled out while me and matey-boy continued our set-to, which probably could have gone on forever, except for the sound of a police siren.

Somebody grabbed me and said, 'Des, let's go'. At the same time, Punchy's boys were doing the same to him and that was it – fight over as me and my mates jumped into the Golf and made our escape. That was the end of that. Or so I thought.

Come Monday morning, I was back at base in Edinburgh when I was told to go and see the sergeant major who was 'upset about something'.

'What happened in Milton Keynes on Friday night?' he asked me as I stood in front of his desk.

He could see my mind whirring. 'Just tell it straight, Des,' he sighed. 'The police have been on the phone.'

'There was a fracas,' I explained. The word 'fracas' was a favourite of mine, one that I knew would cover a multitude of sins.

'Yes,' he grimaced, 'I know there was a fracas. And someone is in hospital after this fracas.'

'I don't know anything about that. It was just a small fracas.'

'Well, it's a fracas that landed some bloke in the hospital, which means you've got to get back down to Milton Keynes police station and sort it out with them.'

As I left, I could hear him swearing under his breath. 'Fucking *fracas*.'

So I flashed the travel pass and hopped on a train down to Milton Keynes, rocked up to the police station. 'My name's Private Derek Powell. I'm with 1 Para stationed in Edinburgh. There was a fracas on Friday night . . .'

I was brought in front of a high-ranking copper, one with his own office, who gave me a quizzical look as I entered. 'No dog collar?' he said.

'I beg your pardon, sir?'

'You're not a man of the cloth then?'

'Come again, sir?'

'Have you got a mate who's in the God-bothering business perhaps?'

'You've lost me, sir. Well and truly.'

'All right. Forget it. Do you want to tell me what happened on Friday night?'

I explained exactly what had taken place. Turned out that some bloke nobody even knew had been on the periphery of my punch-up with Punchy, got knocked to the deck and ended up in hospital.

Did I do it? No. The only person I hit was Punchy.

Did I know who the bloke was? Also no.

It turned out that Punchy had also been into the station to give his version of events, which was the same as mine, and the copper seemed satisfied – so much so that I ended up having a cup of tea with him.

'By the way, how did you know I was a paratrooper?' I asked him.

'One of our boys in the car took the registration of the motor you were in. A Golf GTI registered to a padre in 1 Para.' He stopped. Looked at me. 'Mate of yours, is he, this padre? I'm surprised he's getting involved in this kind of malarkey. I mean, I've heard of bible-bashing, but this is ridiculous.'

I'd almost choked on my tea. *What*? Before it dawned on me. What with the car sale being so recent, the paperwork probably hadn't gone through the system.

'We were a bit concerned,' smiled the copper. 'We were thinking, "Hang on, this is a bit rough. We know them Paras are tough guys, but when the padre comes down to Milton Keynes and starts kicking off down here, it's a bit much."'

When we'd finished chuckling, I said, 'Look, my sergeant major is pretty upset about all this. What can I tell him when I get back?'

'Let's put it this way. Your sparring partner has been in with the same story as you. We haven't had to chase either of you. Neither of you have a record. So we see this as a one-off, never-to-be-repeated deal.' He looked at me. 'Right?'

'Right,' I confirmed.

'Also, we've heard this morning that the guy in hospital is sitting up in bed laughing and joking, so I think we're out of the woods there. You didn't hit him. Matey-boy didn't hit him. I think we're going to let it go.'

I returned to base and told the sergeant major the good news. After that, though, the joke went around 1 Para. 'Have you heard about the padre going down to Milton Keynes, getting pissed and beating people up?'

I used it as my get-out. 'It weren't me. I had nothing to do with it,' I'd say. 'It was the old padre going down and causing trouble.'

This thing got bigger than *Ben Hur*. It sped around the barracks, with people starting to think that it was the truth. Even the actual padre got involved at one point, at first denying he had anything to do with it and then later leaning into the joke, going round throwing pretend punches at people. He got really into it.

Now, if you're thinking, *Hang on a minute, Des. This bloke you've just described who tears it up in Hong Kong, goes taxi surfing, and gets into fights in pubs in Milton Keynes. That's not the Des I thought I knew,* then I don't blame you.

In my previous book, *Bravo Three Zero*, I told a story about a fracas with another bloke while on SAS selection. We had words and I ended up laying him out in the drying room, which is traditionally the place where squaddies sort out their differences. Whatever the barracks, whatever the reason, the drying room is where you go to have a dust-up.

There were no bones broken, but even so, this particular fracas got back to the head shed. I was pulled in for questioning and told in no uncertain terms that punching somebody in the drying room was Para Reg behaviour, and if I wanted to be in the SAS, I had to get rid of that mentality.

It blew up my head. During training, I'd had the Para mindset drummed into me. For seven years in 1 Para, I had lived and breathed that self-same mentality. Anything less would have been considered an insult to my battalion. It was expected of me to be chest-out, tough, cocky and belligerent.

But that was Para. And as I was to learn, the SAS were, if not quite chalk to the Paras' cheese, then very much a different side of the coin. Learning the way of the SAS meant starting again and all the toughness of Para training looking like a walk in the park by comparison.

THE TAKEAWAY

Call it what you want, there's no doubt that the Para 'mindset' is a fiercely combative, never-back-down attitude that serves the unit well in conflict, but can be bit of a double-edged sword in civilian life. I was lucky. I learned that while toughness and resolve are crucial, there's also a time to evolve beyond that mentality, especially when you move to an elite unit like the SAS, where brute force gives way to strategy and diplomacy.

I like to think I always had a bit of that free-thinker in me – my actions on the Sham Chun River speak to that – but it took the SAS to really bring it out in me.

INTERLUDE

Here are two of SAS Regiment founder David Stirling's favourite quotations:

'We are the pilgrims, Master; we shall go always a little further; it may be beyond that last blue mountain barred with snow, across that angry or that glimmering sea'.

'White on a throne or guarded in a cave. There lies a prophet who can understand why men were born; but surely we are brave, who take the golden road to Samarkand.'

– both taken from *The Golden Journey to Samarkand*
by James Elroy Flecker

THE TAKEAWAY

Just to be clear, the above quotes are not the words of SAS founder Sir David Stirling, but come from a 1913 poem that he apparently read while a student at Cambridge. The words became important to him through his work establishing the Regiment and in turn have gone on to inspire those of us who served – including yours truly – giving us an insight into the mind of our founder as well as providing a way forward for us as individuals. To my mind, we are the pilgrims of Flecker's verse, often travelling to foreign lands. We've been sent honourably, as though from a prophet, and as fighters must show steel and courage. That's what those few lines mean to me.

You may find my interpretation fanciful – perhaps it differs from your own – but I sense in those words something of what David Stirling intended when he founded the Regiment, and I take comfort and inspiration from them.

CHAPTER 12

THE ELITE

'It is not in the stars to hold our destiny, but in ourselves'
– William Shakespeare

In a netherworld time between the Paras and the SAS, I sat in the front room of a semi-detached house on the outskirts of Edinburgh with a man I knew only as Smith.

Smith handed me something. 'Here y'go, Des,' he told me as I took it from him and, for some reason, I was reminded of being given my travel pass. I think it's fair to say that this one turned out to be even more significant. What was it? What did he give me? I'm getting to that.

The first time I heard the initials SAS was in the careers office at Bletchley. It was a while later that I discovered what the letters stood for. Not 'super army soldiers' – as declared by Ross Kemp in an episode of *Extras* – but Special Air Service.

Even then, and even though I was myself a member of an airborne regiment, I wasn't especially curious. Having served five or six years in the Paras, I had no firm plans. Maybe go and do something that didn't involve the military, maybe something in fitness. It certainly wasn't the case that I saw myself as a career soldier. Even with all that confidence instilled in me by the Paras, I constantly wondered if I was good enough. They call it imposter syndrome these days. The trial of Para training had long since dwindled in my rear-view mirror. It hadn't yet occurred to me that a way forward might be to test myself again.

My next 'contact' (and I use the word advisedly) with the SAS was while in Edinburgh with 1 Para. I saw a guy on the barracks who wore a sand-coloured beret. His hair was non-regulation length, practically a hippy for the British military. He had week-old stubble and a kind of laid-back, self-assured demeanour. The word I'm looking for here is 'cool'.

I wasn't the only one who thought so. Put it this way, he couldn't make his way from one building to another without having to stop half a dozen times to chat. It looked like everybody wanted a word.

'Who's that?' I said to my mate.

'He's in the death business,' I was told.

'You-what business? *The death business?*'

'The SAS.'

My mate was practically tapping the side of his nose.

'Yeah, they're the elite, right?'

'You might say that. You might also say that they ain't really soldiers. They're assassins, aren't they? Hitmen. Spies, like.'

It was difficult to know whether or not my mate had a low or high opinion of the SAS, but either way, I left it there for the time being.

(Just as an aside, that SAS guy would probably have gone to the

RSM, the regimental sergeant major, who's God in the camp, to introduce himself. I know this because I used to do it myself. I'd go in and say, 'Sir, there's me and a few guys from Hereford on camp, just to let you know. We've got slightly different uniforms on. Oh, and by the way, our RSM sends his best regards.' That way you could just smooth things over ahead of any potential problems because while the young Des Powell was wide-eyed and impressed by the sight of the SAS guy at Edinburgh, there were plenty who found their presence an annoyance and would have no qualms about making that known.)

The third 'contact' was seeing an SAS guy in a ghillie suit, a kind of camouflage suit that makes the wearer look like a bush. I came across him on the range. No jokes about not seeing him, please. He'd chosen a spot away from everyone else to lie down and fire. And there was something about the calm and considered way he took his shots, as though each squeeze of the trigger was of the utmost importance; like the rock star guy I'd seen before, he had an air of being apart from everyone else. My intrigue-o-meter clicked up another notch.

It's always the way. You go from hardly hearing about the SAS to suddenly nobody shutting up about them. I kept hearing about the process of admittance called Selection. Two intakes a year, winter and summer. Just a few men from each battalion allowed to attend.

And how tough it was. I did a bit of reading too. Did my SAS homework. I learned that the Regiment was formed during the Second World War by David Stirling, a Scots Guards officer.

In 1941, as the British 8th Army fought Axis forces, Stirling had proposed the creation of a small, highly trained unit that could carry out deep-penetration raids against enemy supply lines and airfields. Initially, it was called 'L Detachment, Special Air Service Brigade' in order to try to deceive the enemy into believing that the British had parachute units operating in the region.

The SAS's first missions were mainly fails. During Operation Squatter, the unit attempted to parachute into the desert but faced high winds and enemy fire, leading to significant losses. In response, Stirling adapted SAS tactics to focus on overland attacks, using jeeps armed with machine guns.

These raids proved effective, disrupting Axis supply lines and destroying aircraft on the ground. The SAS became a hit-and-run unit: mobility and surprise were their hallmarks, establishing a legacy of unconventional warfare.

After the Second World War, the Regiment conducted jungle operations and once again proved its mettle. As I'd soon learn first-hand, jungle warfare was an SAS speciality. The Regiment's ability to adapt to and master any number of hostile environments was very much a point of pride.

During the Cold War, the SAS operated in the shadows, combating insurgencies and conducting covert reconnaissance, sabotage operations and direct assaults. During this time, the SAS also gathered vital intelligence that informed the larger British military strategy.

Then, of course, came the Iranian Embassy siege, probably the most famous and publicly visible SAS operation, which occurred on 5 May 1980. Six armed men had taken twenty-six hostages inside the embassy in South Kensington, London, demanding the release of prisoners in Iran. After a tense six-day stand-off, the situation escalated and prime minister Margaret Thatcher authorized the SAS to resolve the crisis.

The operation saw SAS operators abseil from the roof, storm the building and neutralize the terrorists within minutes, rescuing all but one of the remaining hostages. The dramatic rescue was broadcast live on television, showcasing the SAS's skill and bravery to the world. This operation not only solidified their reputation as one of the world's premier special forces units, but also demonstrated the effectiveness of their training and tactics in hostage rescue and counterterrorism operations.

And, of course, I learned that the SAS training was renowned for its rigour and intensity, producing soldiers capable of enduring extreme physical and mental challenges, serving as a model for units such as the US Delta Force and the Australian SAS.

And so, perhaps because I instinctively knew that I needed a new challenge in my life, I decided to go for Selection. (And as an aside, it's something I have learned over the years, certainly during my time in the military. There are times in your life when you need to force yourself out of your comfort zone. Chances are you won't have a fairy godmother around to tell you when. The only way you'll know is by listening to yourself.)

But wouldn't you know it? Just as I'd built up the confidence to go for it, I got a posting to go down to Depot and be a physical training instructor. On army bases, you have a guy who deals with administrative matters called an adjutant. I went to see him. I told him my dilemma. I wanted his blessing to blow off the Depot posting and go straight for Selection, but I didn't get it.

'Look, why don't you go to Depot?' he reasoned. 'It'll be a good experience. You'll have everything at your fingertips. You can brush up on your weapons training, hone your fitness and make sure you're in the right frame of mind, totally focused.'

So I took his advice. I went to Depot, screamed and shouted at recruits and failed miserably at the odd bottle jump. At the same time, I boned up on my weapons, tactics and what have you.

I also tried to find out as much as I could about the selection process. *Do your research* is a fine principle to live by, one that applies in all walks of life. Read up. Talk to folk who know the ropes. Pick their brains.

What did I know so far? From my reading up on the history, I knew it was hard. Other than that, not much. I had to rely on talking to blokes who had returned from Selection. And, frankly, those guys weren't giving much away.

Then, one day, I got what we call 'a knock on my bunk', which means that a bloke came to see me in my block.

I'd never seen him before, but he introduced himself as Smith. 'I've heard you're interested in going to Hereford,' he said. Hereford, or 'H', was the colloquial name for the SAS base at Stirling Lines garrison in Crediton Hill, Herefordshire – which, if you've been paying attention, you'll realize was named after Sir David Stirling, the founder of the SAS. (Incidentally, if I haven't pointed out that Depot, aka Browning Barracks, was named after Sir Frederick Browning, commander of the 1st Airborne Division, then consider that oversight corrected.)

'You've been trying to learn about Selection, I hear.'

Word travelled.

'Yes . . .'

'I went on Selection,' said Smith. 'I got as far as the jungle.'

My scant knowledge of SAS selection, gleaned from the

would-be operatives who returned from H, covered the fact that there were three distinct phases: The Hills (which focused on endurance, fitness and navigation); the Jungle phase, a similar unit except conducted in a jungle environment; and then Escape & Evasion, about which I knew literally nothing.

This guy was offering to help for no reason other than the kindness of his heart. He was a married guy living in Aldershot and we arranged to meet, which was how I found myself in the lounge of his semi. The idea, he said, was to bring me up to speed.

Smith told me everything I needed to know, starting with the statement that it was going to be the hardest thing I ever did. He told me what equipment I would need and he told me how to prepare. And then he handed over a small book – a day-by-day diary that he had kept of his three months undergoing selection.

'We started with hundreds of guys,' he said. 'We went to the jungle after about five weeks and we were already down to a fraction of that. We came back from the jungle and we were down to a handful. I say "we", but I mean "they". I didn't make it any further than that, I'm afraid. In other words, Des, if you're going to go for this, make sure you prepare yourself in every single way.'

I was to brush up on my weapons training and to make sure that my fieldcraft was spot-on. He told me that the first phase, Hills, involved just that: 'hills', but also navigation. It remained a key part of the Regiment's selection process because, as was often said, we cannot do what we need to do unless we are fit enough and able to navigate. Fitness and navigation were the bedrock of the Regiment's philosophy and, as I would soon discover, carried right through to the Jungle and Escape & Evasion phases.

I should make sure that, firstly, I had my navigation, compass and map work all squared away. And, secondly, I should see to it that I was fit and good at carrying weight because in the hills phase, I'd start at 40lbs (about the weight of two car tyres or a small bale of hay) and go up to 60 (about the weight of three car tyres). But Smith advised me to prepare incrementally because 'if you go into the hills with anything heavier than 40 pounds, it'll just shred your body, your knees, your hips'.

'Don't worry,' I said, in retrospect a little arrogantly. 'I'm no stranger to the gym.'

He smiled. 'Don't bother with the gym. You might spend a couple of days in and out of there, but after that, you'll never go in the gym again. I'm telling you, work on carrying weight.'

He gave me the diary. He also had a pair of jungle boots that he passed on to me. Jungle boots are made of different fabric, more moisture-resistant, and they tend to come up higher on the leg. These were American jungle boots developed during the Vietnam War. As far as I know, we British didn't have such an item.

I went away with knowledge. And knowledge, as they say, is power. (As a postscript, the diary ended up being incredibly useful, but unfortunately disappeared in mysterious circumstances. I have my theory about where it went but will have to leave it there.)

I look back now and, at the risk of sounding a bit woo-woo, I genuinely think that the universe has a funny way of knowing when you're serious about something and giving you a helping hand in return.

The careers officer, for example. He saw something in me. He saw that I'd be perfect for the Parachute Regiment, and he was right.

Next, Smith, who came up just when I needed information about SAS selection, knocked on my bunk and gave me the information I needed.

Call me mad if you want, but it was the universe telling me something.

I took Smith's advice to heart. First, I enrolled on a two-week mountaineering navigation course with the RAF. A pretty relaxed affair, it involved a bit of going over mountains in Wales carrying weight, but nothing like what I was soon to attempt.

We were taking things easy on the course. But at the same time, I recalled something Smith had said to me that afternoon in his front room. 'As paratroopers, we're used to tabbing, aren't we, Des?'

I had nodded.

'We're good at running ten miles, but that's on the flat. During Selection, you'll be up and down the hills, full packs.'

They call it getting the hills in your legs. Not only did I feel the process begin on the RAF course, but I knew I would need plenty more of it and plenty more endurance as well.

Something else happened that's worth mentioning. A letter arrived for me. Lo and behold, it was from a guy stationed at H, who I remembered as being a very focused individual, a good soldier with a serious temperament. In his letter, he wrote along the lines of, 'I hear you're thinking about Selection. I would certainly advise you to come because I think that life in the SAS would suit you.'

That's what it was. A short letter just giving me that extra little nudge.

At the time, it struck me as slightly unusual. After all, we didn't know each other very well, certainly not well enough to be exchanging correspondence. Now, as an SAS veteran, I understand. That's the way we do things in the Regiment. Interest is noted. Suggestions are made. Approaches follow.

For me, it was another example of the universe talking to me, saying, *Get yourself up there.* And when the universe is talking, you must listen. (And by the way, if you're wondering if Smith was somehow 'sent' by the powers that be, the answer is that I don't know for sure, partly because I never saw him again and partly because I have no real evidence either way. My gut feeling is that he was doing me a solid, and for that, I am eternally grateful.)

Back to my prep. I persuaded the instructors to give me their time and brushed up on my SLR technique and my GPMG skills. Next, I teamed up with three other lads who also planned to attempt Selection and the four of us went to the hills in Wales: the Brecon Beacons, the Black Mountains and the Elan Valley.

There, we started putting on the miles, as well as piling on the carry-weight. I was bearing in mind what Smith had told me to increase the weight in gradual increments and avoid injury. Something else he told me was that the same hills would be used for SAS selection. 'You're already fit, Des,' he had said to me, 'so it's partly about building up your endurance and stamina, but it's also about getting acclimatized. When you reach the summit of a hill, get your map out, have a look around, orientate yourself. Get to know your surroundings. I guarantee you that when you're on Selection, you'll be rushed around so much that you won't take notice. This is your opportunity to get your bearings.'

I was feeling fully prepared by the time my winter slot came up. But before I embarked on four months of likely hell (and that, of course, was only if I stayed the course), I decided that a trip back to Sheffield was in order. Having been shuttling between Edinburgh and Aldershot, I hadn't been home in a couple of years and I wanted to see my family – and to get some roast beef and Yorkshire pudding down my neck. My mum and dad had both passed on, but I had my auntie Elsie and my uncle Pete, who treated me like I was their own.

I wanted it. I needed it.

'You've got all your gear with you,' said Auntie Elsie, eyeing it up suspiciously. I explained that I needed to stay in shape and would be doing some training during my stay. 'Where are the closest hills?'

The answer was that there were no hills close by. What they did have, however, were coal mines, and coal mines have slag heaps.

So that's where I went. I took my Bergen and tabbed up and down the slag heaps for a couple of hours each day.

When I left Sheffield that weekend, my next stop was Hereford.

THE TAKEAWAY

Ahead of Selection, I was taking my own advice. I was acquiring knowledge in order to dispel fear, tuning up, mentally and physically, ready for the challenge ahead. I knew that it was going to be hard, but tried to reduce that big daunting factor by arming myself with knowledge.

That fear will always be there. In a way, it's what keeps you sharp. And when things get loud, fear can keep you alive. But you have to make sure that you are the master of that fear, not the other way around. Doing your research is one way of doing that. Added to the other points I've made, it can be a very powerful tool.

CHAPTER 13

STIRLING LINES

'When you see a strong person, you normally find life
didn't give them a choice'

– Anon

So it was that I found myself at Stirling Lines for Selection.
Hereford may be classed as a city on account of its cathedral,
but in actual fact, it's a small market town. At least it was during
my time. The barracks, which are no longer there, having been
moved to an RAF base, were to be found nestled deep in what
was basically a housing estate. There, at the bottom of a road,
surrounded by normal-looking homes, was the residence of the
SAS, home to the 22nd Special Air Service Regiment and the base
for SAS selection. Most of the selection would take place off-site,
of course. Apart from the Jungle phase, it would be conducted
one and a half hours away in the Brecon Beacons.

For the time being, this was our home.

Bear in mind this was Selection, not training. On Selection,
they let the system fail you. Simply put, the process starts off hard

and gets harder and harder until only the best remain. It subjects candidates to increasing levels of physical and mental stress, and it subjects them to sleep deprivation, which in turn exacerbates the physical and mental stress.

It's a very, very steep learning curve, even for an experienced Para such as I was by then. And when I turned up on that day in the winter of 1985, aged twenty-seven, I felt all the anticipatory pressure of what I knew was going to be a hard road ahead. My first thought was: Thank God I had gone to such lengths to prepare. My second was: Would all that preparation actually mean anything?

The answer would be yes. Yes, yes, a thousand times yes. If you take one lesson away from this book, apart from the lesson on discipline, it's to *be prepared*.

But that was for me to work out later. At the time, standing on the quadrangle at Stirling Lines, it didn't feel that way. I'd felt ready for parachute training. Why didn't I feel ready for this?

I signed twice for the military: once when I joined the armed forces and agreed that I was volunteering to serve Queen and country, and a second time when I signed up for the Regiment, adding my scrawl to a piece of paper on which I agreed that I was volunteering for the SAS on 'permanent active service'.

I remember pausing and looking at that bit, thinking, *Oh, that's different*, before signing anyway. My signature was rewarded with a set of joining instructions that gave me a rough outline of what I was supposed to be doing over the next six months. It had included a kit list, but the kit list, like most else on the joining instructions, was light on detail. My main takeaway from it boiled down to 'bring what you need and make it green'.

As for 'what you need', the unspoken conclusion was that, as a would-be SAS operative, you needed to have worked that out for yourself. Looking back, I know now that anyone who turned up who hadn't armed themselves with as much information as possible, who hadn't been up on the hills and brushed up on their navigation and weapon skills, who hadn't prepared in every way possible, was just not going to get through. It was as simple as that. I suppose you might say that, in many ways, making the information so difficult to come by was the first test. Having had a bit of good luck and the good sense not to look Smith's gift horse in the mouth, I had at least passed that part.

I looked around at my fellow hopefuls. You wouldn't exactly call it casual, but there was no single regulation outfit. Other than 'green', there was no dress code. About half of the guys there were Paras trying their luck in the Regiment, and most but not all had rocked up in what we called our 'working dress': denims and smock.

There were plenty of other units there as well. We had some from the Army, some from the RAF, even from the Navy (though it was more usual for Navy guys to go through Special Boat Service selection) and they wore all kinds of gear – what we Paras called 'go-faster gear': advanced tactical webbing, combat jackets with lots of pockets, boots the like of which I'd never seen before, with gaiters that came up to the knee.

My normal Para contempt for the go-faster sketch deserted me. To me, they looked fitter and more kitted-out than I was. I found myself thinking I thought I was prepared, but these guys look *really* prepared. They looked like Ross Kemp's 'super army soldiers'.

At least I had my jungle boots, courtesy of Smith, stashed

away somewhere. What's more, I'd made a special effort with my regular boots. One of my mates at Aldershot had given me a tip. 'Them hills, Des, they'll give you blisters and your feet will get wet.'

Tell me something I don't know. There's very little you can do to avoid getting your feet wet in the military. Even if your boots were waterproof, the water would get in over the top, and depending on where in the world you were, moisture accumulates anyway naturally. Dry feet are a non-military luxury.

Still, anything you could do to mitigate the wet was fine by me. And I especially liked the idea of avoiding blisters.

'What you do is, right, get yourself a bucket and fill it up with oil. Any oil will do. Cooking oil, cheap cooking oil is fine. Get your boots and soak them in the cooking oil for a week.'

That's what I'd done. In fact, I'd done it in plenty of time prior to Selection because one thing he did warn me was that, for a couple of months after the procedure, cooking oil would still be seeping out of your boots. So, being Mr Prepared, I had indeed gone through the whole thing two months before Selection. But wouldn't you know it, oil was still oozing out of the boots. Not a lot, thank God. Not enough to cause me any problems. But still.

An instructor appeared. He didn't arrive the way instructors are supposed to. He just kind of . . . materialized. He had that SAS 'rock star' look about him. Longer hair. Sand-coloured beret. He spoke.

Spoke, not shouted.

'Welcome, everyone. Thanks for coming on winter Selection here at Hereford.'

He really said that. *Welcome. Thanks for coming.* He hardly even raised his voice.

And that, for me and I dare say for most of them there, was big. It was a huge change from what we were used to. And it was that way right through Selection. We were no longer things to be ordered around. We were treated almost like equals.

Now you might think, *Huge improvement, then, Des?* But 'yes' is only half the answer, because you know where you are when people are screaming and shouting at you. *Get on the wagon. Get off the wagon.* It's as though, by stripping you of your autonomy, your life becomes simpler. You just do what you're told and you do it to the best of your ability.

But right from that very first day of SAS selection, the vibe was one of self-discipline, almost like the instructors were saying, 'Do this if you want. But if you don't want, that's fine too.'

It's deliberate, of course. You're not being trained to operate as a part of a larger unit; you're being prepared to work in much smaller, more targeted groups of maybe even just two or three. After years of being asked to show initiative but only in the context of following orders, we were now being asked to think for ourselves.

'Let me just tell you what's going to happen,' continued Rock Star. 'As of today, we're embarking on the first phase of selection, which is four weeks, including test week. Every evening, the noticeboard will tell you exactly what kit you will need for the following day. During the day, you may be told our plans for the following day, but that does not mean you should fail to look at the noticeboard. Things can change depending on the weather, so at 4 p.m. each day, that noticeboard will contain the most up-to-date information. Hopefully, that's clear.

'Right, here's how it's going to break down. When I'm done talking, you'll take a fitness test. From you, we want to see . . .' He consulted his clipboard. 'Two minutes of press-ups, please. A minimum of forty-five. Two minutes of sit-ups, no fewer than fifty-five, please. And then a 2.4-kilometre run, which you will be required to do in under nine minutes and thirty seconds. Don't worry, we'll go through these times with you again.

'Tomorrow, we'll be doing a short navex off-site, just to gauge your nav skills. The day after that, we'll begin runs in the Brecon Beacons with a loaded pack, and that's what you'll be doing up until test week.

'Now, the Bergen. Next to the noticeboard, you'll see a set of weighing scales. You'll see a hook on the scales. This is where you'll weigh your Bergen. The required weight for your Bergen will be on the board. If you do not have the right weight in your Bergen, you'll be asked to leave. You will also have a list of items that must be inside the Bergen.'

Somebody raised a hand. 'Does the Bergen weight include water?'

'You need to work that out for yourselves. But food will likely add an extra two pounds. Water, another two pounds. You'll also be carrying a decommissioned weapon, another nine or ten pounds. But whatever happens, the Bergen must never fall below the weight stated on the board.'

He went on to tell us that during Week One, we'd be running the Brecon Beacons, adding that 'in order to make the time runs, you'll need to be at a speed averaging four kilometres an hour'. He also explained that we'd complete an exercise called 'the Fan Dance', which takes place on the highest mountain in the Brecon

Beacons, Pen y Fan, which stands at 2,907 feet (886m). Carrying packs the weight of two tyres, our job was to go up it, reach the summit and go back down the other side, before turning around and doing it again – a distance that we had to cover in four hours.

You'd do the Fan Dance early on in Selection to give the instructors an idea of your fitness level, but then you must do it again early on in test week, at which point it would give the instructors an idea of how much you had improved.

He went on. Week Two would consist of navex runs in small groups, as well as night-time tabs with the Bergen weights increasing. We would also be required to carry weapons, as in hold them in our hands rather than on a sling. A seemingly small but actually huge difference, especially when you were climbing.

In Week Three, we'd be doing the runs, which involved making our way to checkpoints, then being given the coordinates of the next checkpoint.

Week Four was test week.

On Monday of test week, the first tab would involve carrying the two-tyres weight. Tuesday, very much the same. Wednesday, same again. Thursday was what they called a 'sketch test', which we'd find out more about later. Friday was the endurance tab or a long drag carrying even more weight.

'One more thing,' said Rock Star. 'Can everyone please look around at each other now? After four weeks, there will be a lot less of you, about a pub-full. After you return from the jungle, you'll all be able to fit in the gents.'

I was looking around, thinking that there were a lot of guys here, three or four pubs-full at least. Nor was it lost on me that this was the winter rather than the summer selection. I'd been told there were double the numbers on summer selection on the assumption that winter was tougher. Me, I'd reasoned that the fewer people there were on selection, the better chance I had of getting through. Plus, I perform better in cold weather. Added to which, I'd heard that timings were slightly increased in winter, whereas in the summer it was said that you had to be a 'racing snake'.

Rock Star continued. 'That's right. As I'm sure you are already aware, we have a very, very high attrition rate on Selection. Some of you will fail because we decide you are not cut out for the SAS. Some of you will fail because your body decides that you are not cut out for the SAS. Most of you will fail because you decide you are not cut out for the SAS.

'If you fall into that last category and you wake up in the morning and feel you don't want to carry on with Selection, do us a favour and stay in bed. Make sure you hand your kit in before lunchtime and make sure you come to the office here and see the boss before you leave and then return to your unit.'

As advertised, we began with the gym session. Shortly after that, our days and many of our nights were spent in the Welsh mountains.

THE TAKEAWAY

With Selection came a feeling of not being good enough to join the ranks of the SAS. I'd heard all these grand things about them, and I was thinking, I can't do that. I could see all these Paras coming back, having failed, and I thought of myself among them, that I wasn't a good enough soldier.

But I remembered another motto that is very applicable to that time: If you want something enough, you'll find a way to do it. If you don't want something enough, then you'll find a way not to do it.

For me, embarking on Selection was a way of testing my own desire. Did I really want this? Did I want it as much as I thought I did? There was only one way to find out.

It's a philosophy applicable elsewhere. Whatever you're doing, if you want something enough, you'll find a way to do it. And if you find a way not to do it, maybe you didn't want it enough. Maybe it wasn't for you, and you should move on and find your bliss elsewhere.

CHAPTER 14

THE HILLS

'Pain that we go through is temporary, but the greatness on the other side is forever'
 – Dwayne 'The Rock' Johnson

Each afternoon, we'd check the noticeboard, which would give us a time to assemble – say, 5.15 a.m. the following morning – as well as a destination –the Black Mountains, perhaps – a weight stipulation for our Bergens and, of course, a distance. Some destinations were better than others, depending on your preference. I especially hated Elan Valley for its soggy terrain, which made the going slow and painful. What's more, you had to be ultra-careful about your navigation or risk accidentally wading into a bog.

Meanwhile, as the days wore on and fatigue bit hard, the weights increased and so did the distances.

Mondays weren't too bad. We'd start off fairly fresh having had Saturday and Sunday off. Tuesdays were worse with fatigue starting to set in. On Wednesdays, the tiredness was really beginning to bite. By Thursdays, we were on our chinstraps with exhaustion. And Fridays were hell.

Every week was like that. By Thursdays, I was running on vapour, but then Friday would come and you'd just about make it to the end. You'd think, *How the hell did I get through that?* Then, on Friday evening, you just go to bed as soon as you got back into the block. Some guys would go home and have a weekend off. Me, I'd stay all weekend, get up late on Saturday and put on flip-flops, shorts and a T-shirt just to let myself air. Then I'd go to the cookhouse and eat as much as I could. I'd do the same on Sunday, preparing myself for Monday, the dreaded Monday, when we'd pull ourselves from our warm beds and dress, shivering, then assemble in the quadrangle where twenty to thirty Bedfords would be waiting to take us the two-hour drive (sleep in the lorry? Impossible) to various checkpoints for the beginning of the exercise.

Guys got injured. They picked up blisters. My toenails turned virtually black and ready to fall off. A lot of others had back injuries, neck strains, blisters on their backs. Some guys, rather foolishly, had applied zinc oxide tape to their backs, hoping to avoid the Bergen blisters. But that tape is vicious stuff. You can't get it off, so when blisters develop underneath, it's murder.

I was one of the lucky ones with my toenails. I remember getting in the shower one day and seeing toenails in the drain. Guys would take their boots off and their feet would be red with blood from toenail loss or burst blisters.

There'd be some days when I'd have fallen over, hurt my back or my back would be aching, or I'd have hurt my neck or done something to my leg. I had to work through it. Unless I couldn't walk, I had to march because the thing that I feared most was the instructor coming up to me. 'You didn't do well today.'

I saw it happen to other guys. I desperately didn't want it to happen to me, but my toenails were a worry. Each morning I put Vaseline on my feet, being careful not to get it on my toes, which I wrapped with tape, then put a civvy sock on over the top, a military sock on top of that, then my boots.

I'd pay extra special attention to lacing my boots (still oozing oil, by the way). Lacing is a personal thing, something you have to do by feel, but getting it wrong can have terrible consequences. Too tight and you'll stop the circulation. Too slack and your boot will slide. There isn't time to stop and sort it out if you get it wrong. The Elan Valley was so treacherous that you'd practically be sinking into the bog if you stopped.

On the hills, they say you must travel at a speed of 4km an hour. We would have maps on a scale of 1:50,000. Grid squares were about an inch, and each grid square represented a klick (i.e., 1,000 metres). If you could cover one grid square in fifteen minutes, that meant you were doing four klicks an hour.

My method was to look at my map, count grid squares and tell myself I had to do four squares in the hour. If I could do that, it meant I was roughly on time.

This was all very well on the flat, but uphill was a much harder prospect. A habit you had to get into on tabbing was striding and surefootedness, creating a rhythm that you stuck to whatever the incline. When you were on the flat, you were doing a little jog. Going downhill, ditto, except maybe faster depending on the surface. Downhill was when I'd try to make up the time lost on the climbs. Prior to attending Selection, a mate had said to me, 'Just take it day by day, Des.' And that's what I did overall, but on these marches, I was taking it hour by hour in fifteen-minute bursts, constantly battling the environment, the elements, exhaustion, the clock.

The point of the timings was to make it to the checkpoints on time. Checkpoints would either be in a valley or on top of a mountain. Either way, the weather would be biblical. With the wind blowing a gale and rain like stair-rods into your eyes, you'd arrive to find a tent pitched there.

It should have been a comforting sight, that tent. It wasn't. The procedure then involved peeling your Bergen off and getting on your belly to crawl inside. They made you crawl so as to keep you uncomfortable. Oh, and to make sure that the tent stayed as warm and weatherproof as possible.

It was almost the same every time. You enter the tent. Inside is an instructor enjoying a flask of tea. He looks at you with an expression of mild curiosity.

You don't get offered tea. Of course not. You're not even allowed to stand up or get to your knees. Even so, it's still better than the fierce weather and soul-sapping tabbing outside.

'Name?' he says, pleasantly.

'Powell.'

He crosses my name off a clipboard.

(I bet that things have changed, and these days he does it on an iPad. But I reckon there's still a flask of tea somewhere in the mix.)

'Got your map?'

Lying there on my belly, I drag the map forward.

'Good. Excellent,' he says. 'Show me where you are.'

The tent has a groundsheet, but I've come prepared and just before I crawled inside, I'd taken a blade of grass from the ground. It's this that I use to indicate my position on the map. You don't do it with your finger. Put your finger on a map, and you're covering a thousand metres, a 'klick' as we called it.

'Excellent. Well done. Jolly good. Okay, now I'm going to give you a grid reference. Show me where that is, please.'

I study the map and with the blade of grass show him my destination.

'Excellent. Now, are you okay?'

'Yes,' I tell him.

'You had better get going then, hadn't you? If you want to fill your water bottles up, there's a jerry can outside. Now off you go.'

And that would be it. For the next three hours, you'd be tabbing to the next checkpoint where the same thing happens again.

'You're a bit behind time, I'm afraid to say. I think you need to get your skates on.'

Off you go again. Keep dragging behind time and you get what they call a Gypsy's warning, something along the lines of, 'You didn't do very well today. You need to improve.' After maybe the third or fourth time of not quite cutting the mustard, you would be told to leave. No big ceremony. No big inquiry. No chance of being back-squadded. You're just asked to vacate your bunk and go back to whatever unit you came from. (That said, everybody is permitted two attempts at selection. It's just that there is no handholding when it comes to whether to reapply. The Regiment says that for the time being, at least, you are not a suitable candidate. And don't forget your go-faster gear on the way out.)

Every day, this was our life. And each day as squaddies dropped out, finding the regime too demanding, there would be fewer lorries in the quadrangle that morning. Guys had dropped out of Para training, but at nothing like the rate they jumped ship from SAS selection – sometimes at the rate of three or four a day. Coming off the back of a six-hour tab over the Brecon Beacons in the dark and freezing cold, they couldn't help but think, *I've got to do this tomorrow and then the day after that and then the day after that.* It wore them down. The thought became too much to bear; mental stress on top of physical hardship. And there was nobody to say to you, 'Come on, Powell, you're doing really well.' Instructors just looked at you blank-faced. Most of the time, they spoke to you politely, like a waiter in a restaurant, creating surreal images of men broken, wet, exhausted and freezing, bent double with the weight of the Bergens on their backs, politely being asked to climb aboard the Bedford for the two-hour drive back to H and just a couple of hours' sleep before the whole thing started again.

The last two Thursdays were particularly vicious. The tab would start at 8 a.m. and finish at around 6 p.m. At that point, having eaten our sandwiches during the day, we would be fed what we called 'airborne stew', which is stew in large pots brought out into the field. Meat mixed with peas and potatoes. It's full of calories, nutritious and easy for troops to get down themselves quickly.

Breaking for something to eat, you'd grab your mess tin, slop out some airborne stew, grab some bread, scoff it down and then set off on a night tab which might start at 8 p.m. or 9 p.m. and then go through to 6 a.m. the next morning. It was torture, the only advantage being that we'd get the weekend off afterwards.

For test week, things were ramped up. As weights and distance increased, the timings shrank, all of it leading towards the final day, which was the Endurance March.

The day before Endurance was what was known as a sketch-map test. The idea was that an agent has passed you a map hastily drawn on a piece of paper, which you had to follow rather than your normal map. I didn't do too well on the test, but fortunately wasn't the only one. We were all so focused on the following day.

Endurance March was like everything linked together, a best-of compilation. It began at 3 a.m., after which it was all-day tabbing, virtually non-stop. Although we weren't supposed to join up with anyone, everybody was going in the same direction, so it was inevitable that small groups formed.

In these groups, opinions would differ as to when it was best to stop, take on food and water, and perhaps have a cup of tea. On a tab like that, you're constantly aware of keeping your energy levels up. You must listen to your body, feeling when your energy drops, when it rises. A cup of tea with plenty of sugar can be a real lifesaver.

Another thing you must be aware of is exposure. This is what the guys at the checkpoints would always be looking for, why they always asked, 'Are you all right?'

It was on Endurance that we were climbing a mountain, with the wind blowing really bad, and I began to feel a bit ill. There was a bunch of us together, five or six, and as we huddled, one of the group said, 'Guys, I'm feeling ill. And if I'm feeling ill, I know there are other people feeling ill.'

He looked around.

'Yes,' I admitted reluctantly, 'same here.'

'Right,' he said. 'We go to the drills now.' This is something we were always taught: if you feel the early onset of exposure, you must do something there and then because otherwise your mind begins to go foggy and you can't make basic decisions. The basic decision in this case was: 'We need to get off this mountain and out of this wind as quickly as possible.'

We trudged on, got to the top and over the other side, at which point we stopped so I could get into my Bergen and get some warm kit on.

My hands were that numb that I had to get one of the other guys to zip me up. I literally couldn't feel the zip on my smock. But it did the trick. All of a sudden, I felt better. And it was a good lesson. Even though we didn't want to take those few minutes to sort ourselves out, it paid off in the long run. Also, we knew to make that decision early.

We kept tabbing for another hour or so until we reached the checkpoint, and there the guy on the mountain who'd admitted he was feeling ill was asked if he was okay, said he wasn't and, rather than them risk having to get the chopper out for him later, he was taken off the tab.

Still, I can thank that guy because it was his thinking that prompted us to get our act together, get some warm clothing on and sort ourselves out. I'm happy to say that he returned a year later and got in.

An important lesson, though. When you feel that early onset, you do something about it. *You listen to your body*. It's crucial in all walks of life, but especially when you're dealing with inhospitable climates. When you suffer from exposure, your body overheats in a last-ditch attempt to warm itself up and you get seriously hot. You overheat. I've heard stories of guys taking their clothes off; another story concerns a guy who started running – out of his mind – and when they caught up with him, he was dead. Your mind goes foggy, gets lethargic and you start to feel drowsy. You fall asleep and never wake up. It's your body going into shutdown mode. This is why the fingers and toes go numb. It's because the body is taking blood from the extremities and bringing it to the core, the important organs, the heart, lungs, and kidneys. You must make a decision early, before it gets to that point. Luckily, this is what that guy did. He probably saved several of us up that mountain. And from the experience, I learned: *Don't dither. Make your decision.*

Aside from that, I almost – *almost* – enjoyed that Endurance March. After all, I knew it was the last one. And I remember coming in and seeing the wagons, the Bedford lorries, which so often represented the beginning of yet another soul-crushing day and actually welcoming the sight of them for once, feeling a wave of euphoria the like of which I'd never experienced before.

By then, we'd been tabbing for twenty hours straight in some of the worst weather imaginable. I could hardly feel my feet, my back was in agony and I had blisters on my blisters.

But I'd done it.

'Powell?'

'Yes, sir,' I managed.

And then they said something they never said – 'Well done' – before adding, 'Now go and get some food in you.' And I pretty much knew I'd passed.

And when it was over, our numbers were way down. Some had dropped out through injury, while most had been deselected and RTU'd – that is, returned to unit – with some given the tap on the shoulder and told that the Regiment had no need of their services. Others failed by not being fast enough, not meeting the timings of test week. And then there were those who purely and simply decided that it wasn't for them. They didn't want it bad enough.

For me, it ranks among the hardest things I've ever done, a constant feeling of up and down. The high? That would be finishing the Endurance tab. The low? It took place on a tab called the Pipeline, a five- or six-hour tab, which, because it was on fairly flat ground, meant I was making good time. All told, in fact, I was feeling pretty good, even though I hadn't seen anyone for two or three hours.

I came to a fast-flowing river and stopped for a moment, remembering a technique we'd been taught for crossing water. Firstly, you take your Bergen off your back and put it on your shoulder because you don't want to fall in while wearing a huge rucksack that's likely to pin you down or pull you under. Secondly, you use the butt of your weapon to feel your way across the river as you turn into the current and take steps across. The idea is to brace yourself against the water, so that it can't take your legs from under you, and to take things slow and steady.

On this occasion, though, I was in no mood to slow down and, what's more, the river didn't look too bad to me. So I did what you should never do. I cheated.

Don't cheat. Don't cut corners.

I kept my Bergen on my back and waded in. Halfway across, with water up to my waist, I realized that it was faster flowing than I'd at first thought. Beginning to worry now, I pushed on, only to find things getting worse. Now the water caught me and

I felt the current pushing and pulling me. The next thing I knew, I lost my footing, overbalanced and fell backwards.

My Bergen pulled me under. I felt it bump to the riverbed. Water passed over me. I kicked my legs but was unable to move. The Bergen was snagged on something.

And somehow the fear of drowning wasn't the worst of it. The cold was worse. Falling back into the river, completely submerged, the freezing cold had grabbed me. It took hold with a grip that sucked the breath out of me, that shocked me with a terrifying intensity. Every muscle in my body seemed to suddenly, agonizingly, contract at the same time. I think that for a second or so I blacked out. It was as though there was a sudden clumsy edit in the film. I saw light through a shroud of water. I could feel myself losing strength, the cold somehow sapping from me the will to live.

From somewhere, though, I managed to summon a burst of strength. Where it came from I don't know. But I was able to pull myself up and, using my rifle, managed to lever myself the rest of the way across the water and to the bank.

And there I collapsed, knowing that I'd just had a very, very lucky escape, an escape I had managed to engineer not out of any particular cunning and guile but out of sheer bloody-mindedness and a refusal to die. That's me, I guess. I'm not the type to go easy when it comes to turning up my toes. With a burst of manic energy, I scrambled to my feet and began screaming and shouting in relief and frustration and anger. I remember looking up at the sky, screaming, 'Don't you fucking dare do this to me. Don't you do this.' I kicked my Bergen like a spoilt little kid.

And then I stopped.

There were three sheep looking at me. Unconcerned, they

watched thoughtfully as yet another cold and wet and nearly dead squaddie lost it on the Brecon Beacons. Nothing out of the ordinary for them.

I thank God for those sheep. Sometimes you need a ruminative mammal to bring you to your senses, to stop you acting like a chump on a Welsh riverbank. *Right, I've got my Bergen. I've got my rifle. I have – thanks to the sheep – got my head together.*

One of the things we'd been taught was that, in the aftermath of a bad episode (and as far as I was concerned, that one counted as a bad episode), you should sit down on your Bergen if you can, have a cup of tea, gather your thoughts, relax and take stock.

So that's what I did. I got my shit together, thinking: *It's a bad day. Things haven't gone right.* (That was just the incident talking, by the way. Things had been fine up until that point.) *No one's going to come and get you. No one knows you're here.* (Which was true.) *And you're cold, there's frost on your clothes, on your beard and in your hair, and to stay alive, you need to get warm. And in order to get warm, you need to get moving.* (Which was also true.) *So get on your feet and get a move on.*

And that's what I did. I pulled myself together. I got to my feet and got moving.

The reason I tell this story is not just because it's a moment of drama in what was otherwise an awful lot of tabbing. It's the fact that pulling yourself together, getting on your feet and getting moving is not only the right thing to do when you're about to freeze to death in Wales, but it's a good philosophy for life.

Either way, it got me through that day of the hills phase and ultimately got me through that whole stage of Selection. Next stop, the Jungle.

THE TAKEAWAY

The Hills phase of Selection wasn't just about physical hardship (although it was quite a lot about that). It was a test of mental resilience. Three of the most important lessons I learned during that time bear repeating: listen to your body, don't dither and don't cheat.

Let's break it down. The physical toll was obvious – blisters, bruised toenails, being absolutely and totally knackered to the point where you couldn't think straight. But what really mattered was how you managed that pain. It was about listening to your body. You couldn't push through blindly, thinking you were invincible.

I remember when we were caught in the wind and freezing rain, and one guy in the group spoke up about feeling ill. That prompted the rest of us to check ourselves, take a breather and get some warm kit on. Ignoring those early signs could have led to disaster, and it nearly did for him. Listening to your body could mean the difference between staying in the game or ending up on a stretcher.

Another of the key takeaways? Don't dither, make your decision. When you're cold, when you're exhausted, your mind starts to fog up and hesitation can be deadly. If you feel something's wrong, take action – fast. On the hills, especially with the clock ticking, you don't have the luxury of indecision.

Lastly, and maybe most importantly, don't cheat, don't cut corners. I learned that lesson the hard way when I tried to shortcut my way across a river, keeping my Bergen on. I nearly got myself killed. Cheating might seem like a quicker, easier option, but in the end, it'll cost you more. The smallest misstep can turn into a massive problem out there. The Hills taught me that cutting corners is a surefire way to end up in deeper trouble than you started in.

CHAPTER 15

LIVE ROUNDS

'As fire tests gold, so misfortune tests brave men'
– Seneca

I did say I was going to talk about weapons training. The truth is that I've never really been turned on by weapons. I think that's the case with most guys in the British Armed Forces. There's more of a gun culture in the US military, but over here, most of the blokes are like me and see weapons as a tool of the trade and little more. What's more, I've come across those who glorify weaponry and, in my experience, they tend to be a bit of a strange bunch. No offence like. If that's your bag, fair enough. Just that, if you don't mind, I'll probably assume you're a bit of a weirdo until I see any evidence to the contrary.

There are, of course, exceptions to the rule, such as those whose interest in weapons is motivated either by their sport or their vocation rather than a kind of fetishistic fascination. I'm thinking of competition shooters, of course. Snipers also. Mostly, if there was somebody in your unit who was overly interested in weaponry, I think he'd be regarded with a little suspicion.

I became quite skilled as a marksman, but it was never something I got excited about. For me, a day on the range was a bit of a boring day. For a start, it was usually Baltic out there on the flat, lying on your belly in the wind. I had quite enough of that during the hills phase of Selection, thank you very much. I was certainly never interested in taking it any further.

Fair play to those who enjoy their shooting, though. In the Army, outside of range shooting, we had combat shooting and competition shooting. Combat shooting is the sort that attempts to approximate a combat situation with moving targets, urban environments, and so on. I'm sure you've seen it in the movies. Competition shooting is more like range target shooting and it's usually via this latter route that squaddies might find their way to sniper school. Here they'll begin to learn more advanced weapon use, as well as camouflage and concealment, how to use the environment, and so on. What they learn is that, most of the time, sniping has nothing to do with shooting at anything; it's about gaining information.

Either way, it was nothing we got involved with during basic training, which of course is where I was first introduced to military weapons. Prior to my time going through Basic at Aldershot, the only time I'd ever seen a weapon was on films and TV. I had certainly never handled one.

Nor did that change as quickly as you might imagine. For a start, it wasn't until several weeks into Basic that weapons training began. Plus, it wasn't as though we lined up and were each handed a gun from a rack. The beginning of our education took place in one of the classrooms and it began with theory, specifically an introduction to the L1A1 Self-Loading Rifle.

Before the L1A1 SLR, British troops had used the Lee-Enfield, which was constructed mainly of wood and therefore prone to damage. The Lee-Enfield was also a bolt-action rifle, meaning the operator fires one shot, works the bolt to eject the spent cartridge and to chamber another round before firing another shot.

It was during the Second World War that semi-automatic rifles first came into use. A fully automatic weapon is one where you pull the trigger and the weapon will shoot until you let go of the trigger. You get very high rates of fire, but low rates of accuracy. Some troops like this. The Russians, for whom an AK47 is the tool, love laying down a lot of rounds indiscriminately for that real 'shock and awe' factor. Traditionally, British and American troops favour accuracy.

A semi-automatic weapon is a halfway house between the two. You get one shot per trigger-pull, but the bolt-action element happens automatically – that is, it's self-loading. Rates of fire are increased – about twenty rounds in ten seconds – and accuracy levels are high.

Semi-automatic rifles became all the rage after the Second World War, when the British Army began searching for a suitable replacement for their Lee-Enfield, which had been in service since the early twentieth century. This search coincided with NATO's formation and their move to standardize ammunition among member nations, leading to the adoption of the 7.62mm NATO round.

Meanwhile, the Fabrique Nationale de Herstal (FN) company in Belgium had developed the Fusil Automatique Léger (FAL), a robust and reliable rifle made of nylon and fibreglass composite that used the 7.62mm round. We Brits liked what we saw of the FAL, but wanted modifications to suit our needs. These included changes to the butt and the handguard, and the inclusion of a folding cocking handle. The biggest change, though, was that although the FN FAL was selective – meaning users could switch between semi-automatic and fully automatic – the British Army decided it was more effective as a semi-automatic only. Therefore, the selector on an L1A1 SLR (as it came to be called) had two settings – safety and semi-automatic – as opposed to three on the FN FAL – safety, semi-automatic and fully automatic. Not only did this simplify the rifle by reducing its capabilities, but it also kept it in line with the British Army doctrine of emphasizing controlled, aimed fire.

The L1A1 entered service in 1957 when it quickly became the Army's standard-issue rifle. Its introduction marked a shift in infantry tactics, allowing soldiers to maintain a higher rate of fire while still engaging targets accurately at long distances. British troops using the L1A1 in conflicts during the Cold War era, including in Malaysia, the Middle East and the Falklands, loved it for its robustness and reliability. It was, as I often say, 'squaddie-proof'.

In the late 1980s, the Army would bid a fond farewell to the SLR. Despite all the ticks in the plus column, there were negatives: not only was the rifle heavy – 9.5lbs – but so was the ammo, added to which it packed a painful recoil. It seemed that thinking had also changed around the use of fully automatic weapons, which is why the Army transitioned to the SA80 family of rifles, specifically the L85A1. Using the smaller 5.56mm NATO round, the new rifle was lighter and allowed soldiers to carry more ammunition. At first, it was unpopular, but after some tweaks, they seemed to get it right.

Me, I'm old school. Having spent years lugging an SLR around in various places all over the world, I can say with some authority that it's a brilliant rifle even by today's standards. Its replacement, the SA80, needs a lot of maintenance and can be tricky to clean. The SLR, on the other hand, only broke down into a few pieces – five if I recall correctly. Drop it or get it wet, it would still work. Nor was it prone to jamming, which many of them are. Like I say, squaddie-proof.

But all that lay in the future. As young recruits in 1977, it was all about that SLR. The instructor began by laying the SLR on the floor and pointing out the external parts. 'Here's the butt. This is the pistol grip. This is the firing mechanism, the trigger. At the top here is the sighting system. This one here at the end is the foresight. This one here closer to the butt is the rear-sight. Coming down, this is the cartridge extractor. When we fire a bullet, the bullet goes that way and the cartridge is extracted out of here. This is the magazine housing. This is the magazine. This is the barrel. This is the flash hider.'

The magazines held twenty rounds. We were shown how to fill them and how to do so quickly, on which we were graded. In those days, you would carry as many magazines as your webbing would allow – four or six. When the magazine was empty, you were to keep hold of it to fill later, unless you were in a high-stress situation where simply discarding the magazine was the most expedient option.

Next, the instructor showed us how to strip and reassemble it, partly to explain how the weapon works and partly to instruct us on cleaning. If you don't have a clean weapon, it will at some point seize up and stop firing, simple as that. Normally this'll take the form of a jam, but it's worth pointing out that a jam can happen for several other reasons, and we were taught through those too: a round not going into the chamber properly or not extracting properly, or a broken firing pin or a misspent round.

Some of these are unavoidable and just down to bad luck – or, occasionally, operator error. Either way, one thing you can predict is that a dirty weapon is an unreliable one, which is why stripping and cleaning was so high on the agenda. We were taught how to vary the cleaning depending on the habitat. Out in the desert, for example, oil will attract sand and, if you get sand in the working parts, it'll seize up. Water, you're all right with most of the time. Not sand.

We were told that each time we took out a weapon in order to, say, visit the range, it would need to be stripped, oiled and reassembled. At the end of the session, the same, and then returned to the armoury (another reason that going on the range could be a bit of a ball-ache).

We moved on to operation – how cocking the weapon was done with the folding cocking handle, which put a round into the firing mechanism. When the trigger is pulled, the firing pin hits the percussion cap at the back of the round. Cordite and gunpowder create gases which force the working parts back, extracting the cartridge and firing the round itself.

This, of course, was very different from the old Lee-Enfield bolt-action method, where the bolt would cock, fire and extract the round all in one. The advantage was that you could fire twenty rounds in ten seconds, but as we were often told, a very loud noise very rarely killed anyone. Accurate firing requires good sight acquisition, which was one of the next lessons: how to point the weapon and line up the sights.

Looking back now, it all seems unbelievably basic, but then you have to remember, firstly, that it *was* 'basic' training. And, secondly, that we were all just kids, really. If you're talking to a bunch of lads whose chief experience of firearms is seeing them on telly, the fact is you've got a lot of reprogramming to do. We were being asked to forget everything we knew, put aside all our preconceptions and start right at the beginning. That's what we did and that's why it took an age – or what seemed like an age – of classroom lessons before we at last got onto the range.

Like I say, the range is not one of my favourite places to be. It's exposed and cold, and because the application of drills is so rigorously enforced (a good thing, I hasten to add), a bit of a faff. More trouble than it's worth, if you know what I mean.

But back then, as young Para trainees, we were absolutely gagging to put into practice what we'd been taught in the classroom. Getting up there, it was doubly exciting to discover that the targets were what they call Figure 11s, which is a picture of a soldier rushing towards you. You have a Figure 11, which is the big one going from the ground, while a Figure 12 is a smaller one which usually pops up from a trench. Each shooter is separated by a distance of 10 to 15 feet, and behind us was the main instructor.

'Okay, with a magazine of twenty rounds, load.' This means you pick up your magazine and insert it into the housing. All the time, we were being watched like hawks. As well as the main instructor, we had other instructors, sometimes even one instructor per recruit, keeping an eye on us to make sure that we observed drills and safety at all times.

And although the novelty soon wore off, that first time on the range with the SLR bucking into my shoulder as I fired off rounds was a rush. For years, right through Paras, in fact, the only weapon I used was that SLR. It wasn't until I was accepted into the Regiment that I was introduced to the M16. (It's worth noting here that we did no weapons training as part of Selection; this was purely when I was a fully paid-up SAS operator.)

The Regiment uses different weapons in different scenarios at different times. For counterterrorism, we preferred to use the Heckler & Koch MP5. This was the weapon used by operators during the incursion on the Iranian Embassy and was preferred because the 9mm parabellum round fired by it was thought less likely to pass through its target and strike and hit a hostage.

The main weapon in use during the period that I served, however, was the M16 and then the shorter, lighter M4. I was glad of that as the M16 was another weapon that I liked. You can trace its history to the Cold War era when the US Army's standard-issue M14 was proving too cumbersome. They looked at the AR15, which in turn evolved into the M16, which took a smaller 5.56mm round and was thought to be ideal for the kind of close quarters combat the US would face in Vietnam. At first, they had problems with it, especially in the jungle environment, but adjustments significantly enhanced the rifle's reliability and the M16 gradually became a beloved tool of the US infantry.

The pivotal moment for the M16 in British hands came during the 1980s. The SAS and the SBS tend to choose their own weapons, and many operators opted for the M16 over the L1A1. The M16, particularly the M16A1 and the shorter-barrelled CAR-15 variant, proved invaluable in diverse and challenging terrain, from urban combat to long-range engagements across rugged landscape.

So even when the SLR was phased out for the regular Army and replaced with the SA80, we in the Regiment stuck with the M16 as our standard-issue and only used the SA80 when we wanted to pass off as regular soldiers. On those occasions, I did use the SA80 and could see exactly why it was unpopular with squaddies. It's a very accurate weapon, but not soldier-proof. The SLR and then the M16, which evolved into the M4 – the 'long' I was using in the contact in that Middle East city described at the beginning of the book – had that pedigree of being refined to suit environments where everything is dirty and wet. All weapons are accurate to a degree. You pick it up, you point it at the target and you pull the trigger. It's about whether the weapon is going to fire when you do so. Will it be rusted? Will it be clogged up? And if it is clogged up, is it difficult to unclog? Soldier-proof trumps accuracy every time. And that's why the Regiment stuck with the M16.

You may be wondering whether I've missed something out. It feels like an important component of weapons training is missing. Indeed, that's the case. It's because I have a story about it. And it involves safety.

Before cleaning, before targeting, the range and everything else, the first thing we were taught after labelling the component parts of the gun was weapons safety. If I were to enter a room today and see a weapon, I'm trained to expect that it's live. In other words, it's got a magazine inserted, full of twenty rounds, with one live round up the spout. It may not have that. It may have some of those things but not all. It may have none of them. But I'm trained to assume that it does.

This is the first rule of weapons safety. Never, never assume that a weapon is safe. It's a good rule for life. *Never assume.* The first thing I would do is pick up the weapon. Next, turn away with it pointed at the ground, check the status of the safety catch and, if it's off, switch it on. Next, I would take the magazine off, cock it three times in order to clear any round that might be in the chamber and dry fire it. Only then, when I'm satisfied that no round is present, will I have made the weapon clear. That is what we call an NSP drill – Normal Safety Precaution. And it's the same everywhere you go in the world, whatever the firearm. So if you were to hand me a weapon, we'd be facing each other and you would go through the NSP drill with me watching you. Only then, when we were both happy, would you hand me the firearm.

There are also strict protocols when it comes to handing out the weapons themselves – in particular, live ammunition when due a range visit. Safety first all the time. We had it constantly drummed into us that using firearms is dangerous; the danger is always present; that peacetime accidents involving firearms are regrettably common and that those accidents happen because of carelessness.

Weapons risk is the most glaring example of something that goes right through life in the army: that army life is full of hazards. In fact, when I joined the Paras, one of the first things I learned was that not only was I stepping into a disciplined life, but also a dangerous one. (The discipline, of course, is at least partly a means of offsetting and reducing the danger aspect.)

In the Parachute Regiment, there was, of course, the parachuting element and there was the trainasium, a fall from which could break an arm or a leg. Then there was the risk of everyday accidents that simply occurred due to the kind of life we led. There are a lot of vehicles involved in army life and I've seen accidents where wagons have reversed into people – or, should I say, squaddies have been standing in the way of reversing wagons. I've seen an incident where an insecure tailgate fell and hit someone's head. I know of an accident where a Bedford flipped over on its way back from the ranges and a couple of guys inside were crushed to death. I heard about a mortar accidentally exploding and killing two or three guys. I've seen a Chinook land and the downdraught flip vehicles onto their sides and on top of a couple of guys. There are plenty of examples where sudden weather has killed people. The events of Bravo 30 are a classic example of that. It snowed in the desert and killed people. It is inevitable that in our business, accidents will happen.

Fast-forward to when I was in the Regiment and when something happened going through training in close-quarters combat in Hereford. The building we used looked abandoned, but with walls that were bullet-proofed with metal sheets and thick rubber.

Why was it bullet-proofed? Because we used live rounds on these exercises. In the Regiment, we did everything live – all scenarios were as real as they could possibly be. This particular exercise was a CT Drill, a counter-terrorism exercise. We had been told that terrorists were inside the house and to expect that hostages would be present. There were five of us entering through the front, another five at the back and a third team elsewhere. In all, fifteen of us were mounting an incursion on a house likely to be full of both hostiles and friendlies.

The bad guys were represented by the larger Figure 11 targets. We would have to expect other targets too. There was one with a guy holding a woman hostage. In some scenarios, targets might suddenly appear and that target might be, say, a child or another friendly. On this day, targets were static.

We wore gas masks, black hoods, black tops, black trousers and body armour. To protect our hearing, we wore earplugs and we were also supplied with Amplivoxes, a radio system that cuts out external noise when you need to listen to whatever's happening on the radio.

The call came through: 'Stand by, stand by.' We tensed. 'Now go, go, go, go.' As soon as we heard that, we burst into the door. We blew the door (I can't give you any details about how we blew the door, I'm afraid) and rushed in. And as we did so, a round went just past my neck.

When somebody fires a weapon very close to you – not at you, just close to you (a very important distinction) – you hear a zip and, at the same time, you feel debris because when a bullet exits a barrel, what's coming out of the barrel is more than the bullet. You clean the barrel of oil, so you'll feel a blast of that, as well as dust particles. And, of course, a bang. All of this happened close enough for me to know that I'd missed getting a bullet in the back by a whisker.

One of the guys behind me had clearly released his safety catch too early, not brought his weapon up and accidentally pulled the trigger.

Momentum kept us coming forward, raising our weapons and taking out the targets until the call came on the radio to 'stop, stop, stop'. We had prevailed. All the terrorists were dead. None of the hostages had been hit. The only victims were the frazzled nerves of yours truly.

People ask whether something like that bugs me. The answer is yes and no, because we must accept that there's danger happening around us all the time. And let's face it, it could have been worse.

I remember the time a guy came out of the training building saying, 'I felt something in my back', and we looked to find that a round had struck him in the body armour. The armour consists of fabric bags with steel plates inserted into them and this particular bullet had hit directly in the middle of the bag. During the exercise, he'd felt something and not thought too much of it until we came out of the house and one of the guys spotted it. If he hadn't been wearing body armour, he would have been killed.

Another time I was at camp and one of the lads pulled me aside. 'You heard what happened earlier? One of the lads on the CT team got shot. He caught a stray round during the drills.' Not only was that guy dead, but the lad who shot him was never the same either.

The fact is that we're in a dangerous business and accidents happen.

The other thing to remember is that, even though they were just exercises, the CT drills were designed to put operators under as much stress as possible. Your head blows up. That's what we call it. Your head 'blows up'. You might have a bang nearby that disorientates you. Things may not be going the way you planned or the way they should. And that's a situation where you rely on – guess what? – your drills.

THE TAKEAWAY

When you do something, commit to it. We had no choice in those elements of training where live ammo was used. In there, we were so close to the edge, so close to death.

What you need in a situation like that is what we used to call a reality check, when you stop to think, What are the consequences here? *You could feel the rounds. You'd see flash-bangs going off. All of this heightens your awareness.*

This is why the drills were so important. Live-round CQB (close-quarters battle) training focuses everything. You need that reality check and you need to be ultra-disciplined. There is no room for error.

CHAPTER 16

IN THE JUNGLE

'No meaningful victory happened without hardship.
Don't bemoan the hard work'

– Anon

Talking of preparation, the next phase of Selection loomed.
'Guys, you're going out to the jungle,' we were told. 'You're all at
the same standard now. From here on in, it's down to whoever
wants it most.'

The reason they chose the jungle was to assess the suitability
of candidates by their ability to cope with the kind of physical
and mental pressure that a jungle environment will subject you
to. Prior to going out, we knew we would be split into patrols,
with each one having its own DS – or directing staff. We'd need
to display good jungle skills, patrol techniques, close-quarter
combat skills and superb navigation, as well as camp and OP
(observation post) techniques. Mainly, we'd need to demonstrate
that, however hostile the environment, we could not only survive
but thrive. And we'd need to do it for a period of several weeks.

It would take a lot of survival. The reason the Regiment used the jungle is because it's a hard and intimidating theatre, a permanently wet, eternally dark and claustrophobic environment. You're in the canopy of the trees. You don't see the light of day. It's hot, sweaty and humid, and everything that lives there wants to bite you, suck your blood, eat you or, at the very worst, take you away somewhere to eat you. There may not be a Predator, like in the Arnie movie, but there are plenty of real-life predators: monkeys that look amazing but are in fact vicious and will attack if they feel threatened, leopards or, if you're especially unlucky, a Siamese crocodile. The foliage gets in on the action too. There's the constant risk of deadfall, where water is soaked up from the ground by dead trees which then fall suddenly, killing the unsuspecting likes of us. And don't even get me started on a particular bush we called 'Wait-a-While', which was notorious for its thorns that hooked into your skin and clothing. You had to stop, carefully remove the thorns and proceed slowly to avoid getting sliced. (Stick around. Wait-a-While is soon to have a starring role in this story.)

There is a flipside to that coin. Another reason that the jungle provides such a good Selection environment, on top of the obstacles it offers, is that it provides a superb test of survival, resourcefulness and initiative. The jungle has everything, if you know where to look for it. It has food, water and shelter. You can dine on boar if you want, but that was only if you managed to kill the boar before it killed you (and, in reality, we lived on ration packs).

Whenever I think about the jungle, I think *claustrophobia*. The canopy trees and foliage are not only all around but above you as well. We used to call it the 'green vomit'. It blocks the light, it seems to stifle the air and it bears down on you.

Navigation in the jungle is a different kettle of fish and therefore was one of the skills we trained in prior to departure – basically, how to move around in limited visibility and how to know where you are when everything looks the same. In a way, you expect that. But what I didn't anticipate was how up and down the jungle would be. Hills everywhere. Moving around was a slow and arduous task. As I was to learn, pacing is crucial. I cracked on to the fact that it took me 127 paces to cover 100 metres, so by counting to 127, I'd know how much ground I'd covered. Understanding contours on the map also required a different approach, since on a jungle map everything appears as an indistinguishable green. It gets everywhere, that green vomit.

Besides navigation, we had to learn (or should that be re-learn) weapon handling, river crossing techniques and jungle re-supply methods. It goes without saying that fieldcraft skills are tailored to each environment and the jungle is no exception. We call them theatres, with each theatre requiring specialized skills. For around a fortnight, there were no exercises and PT was at maintenance levels. We were just learning how to survive in that particular theatre – how not to die in the jungle.

We took two flights to our destination. On arrival, a couple of wagons picked us up and we drove for about an hour to a camp close to the coast. After a few hours of kip, it was time to pack our Bergens before catching helicopters into the jungle.

As soon as we landed, the jungle hit us. I'd looked up as I stepped off the chopper and it would be the last time I saw more than just a glimpse of the sky for weeks. As we plunged into the jungle, that claustrophobia took hold. I had that moment – quickly dampened down, I'm happy to say – of thinking that I didn't like this, that I didn't want to be here.

The RSM and his team had arrived before us to construct a camp and a little school area within the jungle, chopping down trees to make the space that we would, in turn, adapt. The high ground, where helicopters could safely land, had been cleared of trees to prevent the blades from hitting any obstructions. It had taken us about an hour to travel there by chopper. Once a week, it would return to bring us more ration packs and sundry other supplies. Otherwise, we were cut off from the outside world. The walk back to civilization was a mere twelve days.

The first job on arrival was to sort the sleeping arrangements. During training, we'd been introduced to the concept of an A-frame, a sleep structure due to play a major role in our jungle survival skills. The idea was to use our goloks – a type of machete – to create a waist-high structure using poles to form an 'A' shape, with green paracord used to secure the framework and a poncho laid over the top to keep it waterproof. The entire set-up was designed to keep us off the ground, offering protection from insects and other ground-dwelling creatures. And you know what? Done properly, an A-frame is surprisingly comfortable.

Within the camp, we had latrines set up at a designated spot. The latrine is a hole in the ground treated with chemicals to manage waste. We cleared paths for ease of movement between the different sections but, even so, night visits to the latrine required the use of a buddy system for safety. The constant threat of insects and animals ensured that a comfort break was anything but.

So we now had a base camp or 'school'. And within that base camp was a series of smaller camps, one for each patrol. Now it was a case of coping with the jungle, which was in itself a full-time job. It's teeming with threats – creatures that want to eat, bite, sting, or even kill you are lurking everywhere. Snakes that might be in trees or on the ground wouldn't take kindly to being trodden on by a squaddie. Homicidal wild boars might come crashing out of the undergrowth, ambushing unwary patrols. Plus, spiders. Big – really big – spiders. And the leeches. Oh, my good God, the leeches. You needed to be super-cautious of creepy-crawlies, especially the snakes and spiders – constantly checking and shaking your boots and clothes prior to putting them on – because the helicopter was comfortably more than an hour away, so if you got bitten . . .

Hygiene was paramount. The heat and humidity were relentless, which meant we all had a lot of perspiration to deal with. Your pores would get clogged with it, leading to all kinds of problems: prickly heat, which feels like constant nettle stings, as well as fungal infections like crotch rot under your arms and elsewhere. To manage the various rashes, we used nappy rash cream, which was made available near the latrines. You knew when someone in camp had developed nappy rash. They'd be walking around like John Wayne for a couple of days.

To manage all this, we had to practise what we called good field husbandry. Keeping yourself clean was paramount. Washing every day was crucial. At the same time, keeping yourself well-fed and hydrated was key, so we drank water constantly, sometimes with salt tablets to replenish electrolytes. We'd be filling our water bottles at every opportunity – always from upstream where it was clear and flowing to avoid contaminants – and then decontaminating the water with Puritabs. Although they cleaned the water, Puritabs made it taste foul, so we used an orange or lemon powder called Screech to make it palatable. Eating-wise, we lived off ration packs and we always ate as much as possible, but even so, our immune systems were weakened. We all lost weight.

Malaria tablets were another thing. We had to start taking Paludrine a month before heading to the jungle, continue taking it while there and keep taking it for a month after leaving. This routine lasted for three months. A mosquito bite could infect you with malaria and if you didn't have a prophylactic like Paludrine in your system, the malaria could stay in your body, even if you took the tablets while you were there. People had taken Paludrine but still contracted malaria after stopping the medication upon returning home. The virus could remain in the body, and without the anti-malaria tablet to stop it, you'd end up with malaria, despite your precautions.

Clothing could get rank if you weren't careful. We had to wash our clothes while wearing them, rinse off in the river, and then change into dry clothes for sleeping. Keeping dry was important but in practice an impossibility. The only time we'd feel dry – and even then you'd be coated in a thin film of sweat – was in our hammocks, safe in our A-frames at night. Anti-fungal powders like Fuller's Earth helped to dry out the skin, which was vital; otherwise, wet skin would go white, soak up and start to peel off.

At night, we powered down. In a real-world situation, attacks very rarely happen at night in the jungle, simply because moving around is so dangerous in the dark (and you wouldn't believe the night in the jungle under the canopy. It's black. Completely black). Attempting to navigate in the dark would be to risk injury or death, while using a torch was inadvisable because the last thing you want to do is attract predators, be they the enemy or animals. You could trip, get bitten by a snake or fall into a hole, hence the buddy system for latrine visits (you weren't especially popular if you needed the loo at night) and hence why consequently everyone got plenty of sleep – typically from bedtime at 7 p.m. to around 5 a.m., just as it was getting light.

Even so, someone was always on guard at night. It was called 'stagging' – two-hour shifts of keeping watch while others slept.

The morning would usually begin with what else but water-bottle filling. This would be for hydration and for washing. Washing, like the latrine, would be done using a buddy system. One person washed while the other kept watch. We used soap to remove bacteria but never perfumed soap, which was likely to attract insects. The Imperial Leather was left at home. Even the slightest scent could be detected from a distance. It was the same process when it came to dressing for the day. A buddy would watch as we checked our gear for insects before putting it on. I heard the tale of a bloke who found a Borneo pit viper in his denims.

Next came breakfast – whispered conversations, tea and porridge – from which you'd have to clear up impeccably. Our DS would be around and if there was any mess, we'd be penalized for it.

After that, we'd usually go on patrol. Patrolling involved a lead scout who'd navigate and alert the patrol to potential dangers. We'd be stopping for navigational checks to take on food, our senses attuned to the jungle as we noticed things that initially we'd missed. For example, you might be making your way quietly through the jungle and stop to bask in a small shaft of sunlight that has penetrated the canopy, but as we gained experience of jungle survival, we learned to be wary of those slivers of sunlight. Snakes liked to bask in them, too.

We also learned to listen to the jungle. We were constantly listening for the sound of deadfall and, if the jungle were to suddenly fall silent, we'd know that a big predator was hanging around – one of the clouded leopards they have out there, perhaps.

Back at camp, we'd have what you might call schoolhouse lessons. We'd practise tactical drills and carry out exercises – anything to test and challenge our soldiering skills.

Occasionally, we'd have some interaction with the local tribes. They'd only started encountering civilization in the last few decades, but in that time, the Regiment had developed a good relationship with them, inviting them to teach us jungle tracking and survival skills – the very same skills that had been passed down through generations. Using sign language and very basic communication, the tribespeople helped us understand how to navigate the jungle, find food and use natural resources effectively. They taught us how to prepare and preserve food, as well as showing us how to smoke meat to prevent it from spoiling.

And then, as darkness fell around 6 p.m. – the canopy causing light to fade rapidly – we'd go into our evening routine, using head torches for cooking and discussing the day's events, learning lessons and preparing for the next day. Getting ready for bed was – to coin a phrase – a military operation and involved changing clothes from very wet ones to slightly less wet ones (but always wet), checking for creepy-crawlies, getting into bed and, at last, to sleep. By 7 p.m., we were in bed getting much-needed rest.

I quite enjoyed it all told. Two weeks down, I was in the groove and had no worries about staying the course.

Not until the shit hit the fan.

It happened on a drill. While out there, we were taught essential drills known as close-quarter battle drills. The drills were designed to simulate real-life combat scenarios where encountering the enemy could happen at any moment, including ambush scenarios. As with all exercises in the Regiment, close-quarter battle drills were conducted with live ammo, which made it crucial to follow strict rules about where and when to fire.

Instructors monitored us from behind. As we patrolled in single file, the front man would be the first to spot any targets, indicating enemy presence. On sighting a target, he'd shout 'Contact front' and open fire. We in the patrol would then spread out and engage the enemy, while simultaneously extracting ourselves by moving backwards, firing and retreating through dense foliage.

This foliage included the Wait-a-While bush. Remember that? The bush with the razor-sharp thorns . . .

We moved along the contact lane at a clip. As we did so, targets appeared unexpectedly from the foliage, some hidden in the undergrowth, only visible from certain angles, some attached to trees. The key thing with the drill was to resist indiscriminate firing. We were to open fire only at visible targets and, if there was any doubt, hold fire.

'Contact front,' came the call. Our M16s went to our shoulders as we looked for targets. At the same time, we started running.

I saw a target in the trees. Pop pop. Around me, the patrol was getting rounds off, all on the move.

I felt something snag my arm, but didn't think too much of it. A scratch from the undergrowth maybe. I had bigger fish to fry. But as the contact ended, I glanced at my arm and saw blood there. At first, I thought, *God, I've been hit by a stray round.* I knew that the pain of a gunshot wound can take a while to register.

But no, it wasn't that. On inspection, I could see that a thorn was in my arm. I grimaced, thinking that I knew a Wait-a-While thorn when I saw one. I hadn't waited. And look what had happened.

'You all right, mate?'

That was Special Needs out of my patrol.

'Yeah, Spesh, it's nothing. Just a little scratch.'

'Doesn't look like nothing. Looks like you've gone and hurt yourself there, Des.'

By now, blood was leaking out of my sleeve and onto the jungle floor. My newly acquired jungle survival instinct told me that the resident nasties would soon be feasting on it, but that was the least of my woes. Investigating the wound in more depth, I could see that the thorn was deep into the flesh. When I tried to pincer it out with my fingertips, it wouldn't come.

We trooped back to camp, where the DS and Special Needs fetched our medic. Seeing my wound, he sucked air through his teeth, pulled a face and reached for a pair of impressive-looking tweezers, muttering about infection as he tried to pull out the spike. No go.

He was talking about the worry of hitting a blood vessel,

making a bad situation worse. There was further mention of possible infection. Up to now, I'd been thinking it'd be a case of patching me up and sending me on my way, but the medic was behaving like it was far worse than that. Special Needs had fixed me with a look that every hurt soldier dreads: sympathy.

The medic and the instructor had a conflab. Between them, they decided that I would need to be medevacked to mitigate the risk of infection or further complication.

'Oh, come on . . .' I was saying. 'Really?' I was thinking that if I left the Jungle phase after only two weeks, then surely I'd fail it. And if I did that, then surely I'd fail Selection altogether. All that time tabbing on the Welsh mountains. Two weeks of being wet and hot and besieged by insects in the jungle. For what? 'Ta-ra, Des. You're out of the programme through no fault of your own.'

My protests fell on deaf ears. There was no other option, they said. A helicopter was called.

'They can patch me up and I can return though, right?' I said to the blasted medic.

He pulled a pained face. 'Better pack your Bergen,' he said. 'Just in case.'

With a heavy heart, I did as advised.

From the camp, I was taken to the medical centre, where they took an X-ray of my wrist, oh-so-helpfully confirming what we already knew – the reason I was there in the first place – that there was a spike embedded in my arm. One small procedure and the introduction of some antibiotics later, I was thorn-free and making noises about getting back into the jungle.

No, they said; words like 'complications and 'observation' were used. They explained how the jungle was a dirty environment full of potential infections (I didn't bother arguing that particular point) which could turn a small injury into a significant medical issue. They cited cases of other guys who'd suffered severe infections from similar injuries. Ultimately, they made the decision for me and I was put back in my box.

The camp was about half an hour's drive from the med centre and so that was where I washed up, moping around the place, being 'observed' and trying to keep my mind occupied with food and the mundane routines of camp life as I waited for Special Needs and the rest of them to return from the jungle.

'How's the wrist, Powell?' said the DS, when they eventually showed their faces. He looked at it. 'Looks all right,' he said.

No consolation.

'You can come back,' he said, as he clocked the look on my face. He gave me a meaningful look. 'We'd *like* you to come back.'

The guys who had been out in the jungle had a day to rest and regroup. We had a curry together, but by 6 p.m. most were getting their heads down. Early next morning, we were up around 5 a.m. to load our stuff onto lorries. We headed to the airport and flew to the nearest major city, where although we had the chance to go out and enjoy ourselves, most were too tired (or in my case, too pissed-off) to bother.

The next day, we flew back to Hereford, arriving on Thursday evening. The following morning, we assembled in the lecture theatre. This was the moment of truth: when they announced who had failed and who had passed. They called out names, mine included, and we had to go into the next room where the announcement was short, sharp and to the point. 'You've not got through.'

Six months later, though, I was back.

THE TAKEAWAY

The Jungle phase was all about survival, and one – maybe THE – the biggest lesson I took from it was this: you've got to nail the basics. If you don't get the fundamentals right in the jungle, you're done for. And when I say basics, I'm talking about things like hygiene, staying dry (or at least as dry as you can), keeping your gear in order, maintaining your sleeping area in good order and so on and so forth.

In the jungle, everything's out to get you – leeches, snakes, even the air itself. It's hot, wet and suffocating. You can't control that, but you can control how you respond to it. Wash yourself. Stay on top of hydration and nutrition. And do it all the time, day in and day out.

It's the same in everyday life. You can't control the world, but you can control how you handle it, how you respond to it. If you don't take care of yourself – eating properly, getting enough sleep, handling the admin of daily life – it all adds up. The small, routine tasks matter. Whether it's work, family or just getting through the day, master the fundamentals. If you skip those, the bigger challenges will trip you up.

So, yes, lesson learned: in the jungle and in civvy life, it's the basics done right, day in, day out, that keep you going.

CHAPTER 17

BACK TO THE GREEN VOMIT

'Show me a hero and I'll write you a tragedy'
– F. Scott Fitzgerald

Getting stabbed by the Wait-a-While bush, and then being canned because of it, was what you'd call a stroke of bad luck. I wasn't discouraged by what had happened. Quite the reverse. It lit a fire underneath me. Remember that drying-room incident I mentioned earlier? This happened around that time. A bloke got me riled up and, one visit to the drying room later, a Para mentality that I really should have left behind re-emerged and I laid him out.

That drying-room punch (not quite a fracas, if you're wondering about the absence of that word) was one of the subjects under discussion when I went to talk to my superiors about having a second go at Selection. (And, of course, a final go; you're only allowed two attempts.)

I wasn't allowed to come back for the very next intake. In fact, I was advised to wait a year.

'With respect, Boss,' I'd said, 'I'll lose momentum. I want to come straight back while I'm keen, ready and in the right frame of mind. I feel I can do it. I was unlucky this time.'

He looked at me. 'Well, okay. If your mind's made up – and I can see that it is – I'll put you forward.'

This particular major knew the score. He knew me and what type of guy I was.

Leading up to my second go-round at Selection, I did the same training and build-up as before. I knew the routes, which gave me an advantage prep-wise. The disadvantage was that I'd built up a bit of fear. I couldn't afford to flunk Selection again. I certainly didn't intend to fail on account of my own shortcomings. But what if I was the victim of bad luck second time around? What if the Wait-a-While bushes of the jungle got me again?

But I got on with my prep. Up the Welsh Mountains, down again. I embarked on Selection again and I did the Hills again. And the Fan Dance, the Pipeline, Endurance and the rest. Again, it helped knowing the routes. Kinda. The disadvantage was psychological. I knew how hard it was going to be.

But I did it and once again came through Test Week and Endurance.

Returning to the jungle, I found myself back in the groove. We did the same lessons and sometimes instructors would have a bit of fun by saying, 'If you want to know what's happening tomorrow, go and have a chat with Des.' And, sure enough, the guys would come to me to ask what was happening and I'd at least be able to tell them what happened last time.

One incident worked in my favour. At base camp, after a day's training, the instructors would suddenly fire shots in the air and yell, 'Attack, attack!' You had to grab your kit and extract yourself.

The first time, it was a complete surprise, but the second time, I had a feeling gleaned from my previous experience that it would happen around the same time. I told the patrol to have their kit ready, just in case. Sure enough, when it happened, we were prepared.

One of our tasks was jungle resupply, which involved choppers bringing in food, weapons, ammunition and other supplies without landing. There was a landing area nearby, on the other side of our camp, but it was generally only used for picking up or dropping off personnel. Everything else would be winched in through the canopy. The chopper crew got coordinates giving them a rough idea where to offload the gear, but of course there were very few landmarks in the world of the green vomit. So, to tell the chopper exactly where to hover and winch, we used a location-marking balloon.

Made by a German firm, the bright-orange location balloon – a huge thing with cords attached like a kite – arrived in cardboard packaging. Also contained were blocks of chemicals, similar to firelighters which, when mixed with water, produced gas to inflate it, taking it up to bobble above the canopy and let the crew know where we were.

We would practise this, with each patrol taking it in turns to use the balloon, adding water to the crystals and watching it rise, all timed by instructors, after which, we had to clean up. On this occasion, which – important detail alert – was mere days before the Jungle phase was due to end, we were doing it for real. We raised the balloon. Our goodies descended through the canopy and some of the lads began to sort them as I turned my attention to the task of clearing up.

'Grab that, would you, Des?' came the shout as the rotors blatted the air overhead and I started pulling all the balloon crap together, ready to deposit in one of the black bags we would take with us when we left. (As an aside, we would leave no trace of our camp, nor did we ever find any evidence of previous camps.) I stooped, scooped up all the stuff and squishing it all together, shoved it into one of the black bin liners.

Job done. Thought no more of it.

A few moments later, I felt a heat on my left thigh. To be honest, it was quite pleasant at first, a bit like applying Deep Heat. Moments later, the heat had become a burning. Like, an actual, painful burning. I looked down at my denims, thinking it was odd but that it would go away. Like maybe I'd just been snagged by some foliage.

But it got worse. Really quite bad. A patch had appeared on my denims and it was suspiciously white and corrosive-looking. The same white stain had appeared on my boots. My thigh was burning intensely now. Thought of the Wait-a-While incident bubbled up. I alerted the instructor who called over the RSM.

'What is it, Powell?'

'My leg's burning, Boss,' I said through clenched teeth, my pain intensified by a creeping, horrible sense of history repeating itself.

The RSM wanted me to pull down my trousers and it was one of those situations where nobody was making jokes as I yanked them down and stood there, wincing, unable to look down at my own thigh because his face told me everything.

It was bad.

No doubt you've come to the conclusion that we reached. Chemicals from the balloon had leaked onto my leg. What a time to discover that said chemicals had a caustic effect when they came into contact with the skin.

And would cause intense pain.

Check.

Followed by blistering.

Also check.

A boil had already started to appear. Like something from *The Thing*, it had started to spread. I swear I saw it pulse.

And yet, despite the pain, the main thing on my mind was the fact that I was so close to completing the Jungle phase and now . . . *this*. And it was clearly bad – bad enough that the RSM and the medic, after quickly conferring, had decided that we needed to call the chopper back.

Like I say, some of the stuff had got onto my boots, so I had to take those off, too. Off came my underpants. All I wore below the waist was my socks. And apologies that I'm not playing this scene for comedy because, despite the full-frontal male nudity, it was a bad, bad scene and I was properly distressed as I scrambled back to my basha to grab my Bergen and my weapon.

By the time I'd got my shit together, the helicopter was back, and all was noise and storm as it sat there turning and burning, awaiting my appearance. I put my boots back on, stuffed my trousers beside my webbing belt and, with only my shirt on, ran up the hill, holding my stuff.

I approached the chopper from the front, kneeling to indicate to the pilot. You must do this to let the pilot know you're entering. If the ground is uneven, there's a chance you could get hit by the blades, so you must let the pilot see you.

I then went around the side of the chopper, entered through the side door. The Loadmaster, who helps with equipment, was talking on the mic, probably about me with no trousers on. Everybody wore slightly bemused expressions. You can't blame them. I was just thinking . . .

God, what was I thinking?

That's torn it.

Here we go again.

Another fail. My last chance.

At the same time, and being a bit of a glass-half-full type, I thought to myself, *Is it going to make any difference?* After all, there were only two days of Jungle left. I'd either done enough or I hadn't. Surely, they wouldn't see this as a fail . . .

The med centre, which was the same one I'd been to with the thorn in my wrist (if only they did a loyalty card scheme), had been told that a burns victim was coming in. Bonus – they got a naked burn victim. Doctors confirmed it was a chemical wound and sprayed what was by now an impressive-looking blister with ice-cold coolant. I was given morphine and antibiotics, and suddenly the world looked a lot better.

A couple of days later – and at least there wasn't much of an agonizing wait this time – the rest of the lads arrived back from the Jungle, and I endured several rounds of 'Unlucky, Des' before we were on a plane back to Brize Norton and then to Hereford.

The following morning came the familiar meeting in the

lecture theatre. The sergeant major called out names, including mine, and we were told to go to the next room.

There, the wait was interminable, until finally, an instructor walked in. 'Congratulations guys, you've got through to the next stage. I'd like you here tomorrow at 9 a.m. when we start Escape & Evasion. Off you go.'

For the remaining lads in the lecture theatre, the news was not as good. The sergeant major would have told them that they'd failed. A brutal process. I'd been there before, hearing that I hadn't made it. The message was always blunt: 'Unfortunately guys, you haven't got through, you've all failed. Go back to the block, hand your kit in and we'll have you away by lunchtime today.'

There was no room for argument. Failure was final.

THE TAKEAWAY

In the jungle, discipline is a way of life, a lifeline and lots more besides. The smallest slip in routine can cost you dearly. Of course, you don't want to check your boots for snakes every morning or wash your clothes in the river again, but you do it. Discipline means not wanting to do something but doing it anyway. And that same discipline keeps you sharp and ready for anything, no matter how tired, wet or fed up you are.

The Jungle phase drilled this into us, but it's not just crucial for survival in the green vomit. In civvy life, the same principle applies. Whether it's sticking to a fitness routine, turning up to work even on the bad days or getting through those tedious tasks, discipline is what keeps everything ticking over. It's about pushing through dis-comfort to get the job done, knowing the payoff comes later. Without it, you lose your edge. In the jungle or in day-to-day life, letting things slip can lead to bigger problems down the line. Maintaining that discipline, doing the routine, even when you really don't want to, is how you get through it – whatever 'it' may be.

CHAPTER 18

HELLO DOLLY

'Women and children sleep safely in their beds at night because rugged men are willing to do violence on their behalf'

— George Orwell

During my time in the jungle, I ate my fair share of unusual grub. Snake, monkey and wild boar were all on the menu at one time or another. Jungle squirrel? Yup, I've had it. It wasn't the tastiest, but it provided the necessary sustenance, and it did at least make a change from the endless ration-pack food. In desperate times, even insects are fair game. Praying mantis for dinner? If you must. (I didn't, if you're wondering.)

It's fair to say that out in the jungle we had a bit of help when it came to what you might call the local cuisine. Our instructors were on hand for advice, while the tribespeople we met were particularly helpful in that regard. They were the ones who showed us how to smoke the meat that was crucial for preservation, giving it a barbecue-like taste while extending its shelf life. (And when you consider that boiling the meat is the most reliable way of making it safe to eat, smoking can also add some much-needed flavour.)

Those guys were great with the golok, or parang machete, which I mentioned previously, a type of machete shaped to create more cutting power with a simple flick of the wrist. They showed us how to cut bamboo and rattan, a strong vine that could be used like rope. Building shelters was something that went into the skill-box, thanks to the jungle.

We were about to add to those skills, especially those that involved hunting, fishing and killing our own food. Welcome to the Escape & Evasion phase of Selection.

Like most other aspects of Special Forces Selection, Escape & Evasion has changed over the years. In my day, it was simply Escape & Evasion, followed by Resistance to Interrogation, so that's what I'm going to talk about.

It lasted four weeks, with the first three dedicated to training. The final week would be spent alone and on the run with only the most rudimentary equipment and, for some reason, dressed in the oldest, scratchiest Second World War clothing they could lay their hands on. Six or seven nights of living off the land and evading a hunter force operated by the Paras, after which we'd be captured, whether we liked it or not, and interrogated.

We'd all heard horror stories about that bit.

We began in Hereford for the theoretical part of the training. The lessons were based around the idea that there are various possible scenarios you might find yourself caught up in. A drop may have gone wrong, leaving you way off course and lacking in support.

Or you might be on patrol and suddenly find yourself alone after an enemy contact, split up from your team and without your essential equipment.

Or you might have been briefly captured but been able to make your escape and now needed to live off the land while staying one step ahead of the bad guys. How do you do it?

In essence, the goal was to prepare us for any situation in which we might be isolated and pursued by the enemy.

Well, I say that was the goal. It certainly was in theory. But although we were sponges, soaking up all the training we could get, we remained focused on that final week when we'd have to go on the run, with virtually no equipment, no compass, no food, no laces in our boots or belts in our trews. Just a tobacco tin with a Durex in it (I'm only half-kidding, as you're about to discover), our wits and our training.

On Monday morning, we gathered – those of us who had survived Selection so far – along with guys from various other regiments.

To me, it felt like you could tell the two groups apart by sight. There was a distinct difference in how the regulars carried themselves compared to us. They hadn't been tested in the same fires and it was just ... *evident*. Don't ask me how. You could just tell.

For the other blokes, this course was voluntary but prestigious. Passing it would be a feather in their cap. Meanwhile, instructors had made it clear to them: they were to leave us SAS candidates alone. We were part of our own continuous training and they weren't to interfere with us or bombard us with questions.

The lessons began, some of them in lecture theatres, some in the field and some in the cookhouse. Most of the lessons were taken by instructors, but for some we had veterans who'd been captured during the Second World War and other conflicts. My God, they had some harrowing stories, full of lessons learned the hard way: one had been held in Colditz, another by the Japanese during the construction of the Burma Railway – *The Bridge on the River Kwai*. Their experiences added a grave reality to the theoretical knowledge we were gaining.

What did we learn? You'll appreciate that we're talking about a highly secretive organization here, so I can't and won't go into all the tradecraft. But here's a selective rundown.

FOOD

Food is vital in a survival situation. It provides the energy you need to keep moving, to stay warm and to think clearly. While you can survive longer without food than without water, a lack of nutrition will quickly sap your strength and morale. Knowing how to find food can make the difference between life and death.

Lessons began with the basics of how to identify and catch edible animals in the wild, identification being key. For the purposes of the exercise – which would take place where else but in Wales (although of course weren't told where) – we learned about the only two breeds of snake indigenous to the UK: the adder and grass snake.

We were told that if you come across a snake, don't provoke it.

But if you have no choice and need food, you can kill it, cook it and eat it. Just be careful while you're at it.

The grass snake is harmless, but the adder can be poisonous. Its bite isn't usually fatal – the last time we had an adder-bite fatality in the UK was sometime in the 1950s – but it can be dangerous if you don't get treatment in time.

In civvy life this means *don't panic* – an important edict at all times in everything you do. Stay calm, immobilize the bitten area and get to a hospital for anti-venom treatment. It's not a death sentence – not like the fer-de-lance in Australia, which can kill you within minutes – but it's serious.

As for cooking a snake, you slice off the head, where the venom glands are found. You need to be careful, because the head of a venomous snake, even chopped off, can still bite you, as they have heat-sensitive areas on their face which will react automatically. Next, you cook it in its skin in the embers of a fire. When the skin splits, the meat is ready to be scooped out and eaten. I'd recommend boiling it first, but then, as you're about to discover, I recommend you boil everything.

Frogs are another reptile you can eat. You need to skin a frog first. They often have toxins in their skins. And they're best cooked on a stick.

What became clear was that we were being taught to understand and utilize the ecosystem. If you're doing it properly, you should be hyper-aware, looking around you all the time, whether that's for navigational reasons (keeping track of landmarks), or for scavenging and foraging reasons.

Those animal droppings over there? The ones you'd never

normally notice. Do they indicate the presence of a run, which are the well-trodden paths that animals regularly use? Can you therefore set a snare along a run and catch yourself a rabbit?

We were shown how to do exactly that. A snare is basically a bit of wire – usually brass wire, a length of two to three feet – that you can use to trap smaller animals. In the case of catching rabbits, you place your snare along rabbit runs at night, go and have a kip, and by morning, the chances of catching one are high.

Say if you catch a small rabbit, it might be worth using it as bait to try and catch something bigger, again by being able to identify runs from droppings and tracks. The captured rabbit will jump around, make a noise and attract bigger predators, but you're the biggest predator – or you hope so.

And when you get a bigger animal? I could fill a book with the ways in which to skin and cook rabbit, badgers and foxes, but the short version is that literally nothing goes to waste. It's not just the meat you eat. Liver, kidneys, lungs, even the stomach – all can be eaten and all will give you essential nutrients. The important thing is that they're thoroughly cooked.

That goes twofold when cooking a carrion-eating bird – crows or ravens, for example – so you have to be sure to boil it, which is the best way to make it safe (and also the best way to make it taste disgusting, but needs must).

Having said all that, liver can be eaten raw if necessary. It'll taste horrible but contains lots of essential nutrients. When it comes to the lungs (the lights), you'll need to check for any mottling, which might be the sign of respiratory disease in the animal. Intestines will need to be boiled. Tail, feet and bones can be boiled to make soup. The cheeks make good meat-flesh. The tongue is highly nutritious. The head can be boiled.

Nor, of course, should you neglect the pelt. We were shown how to skin an animal in such way that its pelt would be retained and used for warmth. Everything has its use.

(And those droppings, by the way? Dried out in a bag or pocket, they can make good fuel for the fire, which could be invaluable if you're operating in wet conditions.)

The long and the short of it is that on the one hand you can eat an awful lot of what you can find and/or hunt, but on the other hand you still need to be careful. We've all seen Bear Grylls on TV, eating maggots and other questionable items. While it makes for great television, it's not something you'd actually do unless absolutely necessary.

Similarly, the contestants on *I'm a Celebrity, Get Me Out of Here!* are often forced to eat things for the shock factor. But in real survival situations, eating such food can be dangerous. If you scoff something bad and end up vomiting, you become dehydrated and lose precious energy. That's why you must stick to basic, safe food and clean water when you're out in the wild.

A key part is knowing the difference – recognizing whether the food is safe to eat. We were taught that if you come across a dead rabbit, vole, weasel or fox, it's generally not safe to eat. The meat could be off and consuming it could lead to diarrhoea or food poisoning.

Next – and vegetarians look away now – they brought in a sheep.

The instructors were like, 'Gather round, come and meet our

new friend. Her name is Dolly.' And for a brief deluded moment, I thought, *Phew, they're not going to kill the sheep.*

And then it dawned on me that this was the SAS. And we were learning how to survive in the wild.

Of course they were going to kill the sheep.

No, of course not. Not 'them'. They'd make one of us do it.

A cute-looking sheep, she was. Poor old Dolly. I can't have been the only one thinking what I was thinking. Like, *Really? Honestly? Is this actually going to happen?*

'She's a lovely one, aren't you, Dolly?' said the instructor, tickling her under her chin. In response, Dolly let out a plaintive little *bah*.

'Let's have you up here, then,' the instructor told us. 'Come meet Dolly.'

You evil git, I thought, as we all gathered round like kids on a farm-park trip, giving Dolly a stroke. 'Get to know her,' added the instructor. 'Go on, she won't bite.'

'*Bah*,' said Dolly.

And I'm sure it hadn't escape anybody's notice that on the demonstration table was a sharp-looking knife.

We retook our seats. 'Which one of you is going to do it then?' asked the instructor equally.

If some guy had thrust his hand up and bounded forward, dead keen to slit the poor sheep's throat, he would probably have failed Selection. The Regiment doesn't want people like that.

Now, the whole sketch wasn't entirely unexpected. I'd heard about this process from other soldiers. Apparently, they usually picked on an officer. Even so, we were all looking a bit shifty, regardless of rank. Not wanting to be picked, not meeting anybody's eyes. Nobody wanted to be the one.

And they looked at the officer.

I should explain that on Selection were officers, who did everything that we did, with the addition of the infamous Officers' Week. This was a gruelling test of endurance and capability that took place after the Jungle phase of training. Officers were given a series of demanding tasks that tested their abilities to handle pressure and make critical decisions.

One of the tasks involved writing up orders for a reconnaissance mission, known as a 'close target recce'. A sergeant would volunteer his house for the exercise. The officer was instructed to conduct a recce on this house in the middle of the night, around 3 a.m. The sergeant, playing his part in the scenario, would be out in the garden, pretending to hide weapons in the shed. The officer conducting the recce would have no prior knowledge of the sergeant's identity and would need to observe and report all activities accurately.

After completing the recce, the officer would have to return, write up his orders and be ready to present them by 8 a.m. This presentation would take place in our lecture theatre.

It wasn't just about the orders. The instructors would rip the presentation apart, questioning everything to see if they had potential. They'd ask, 'Have you thought of this? Have you considered that?' It was a test of whether he could deliver orders, take criticism, handle the stress.

I've been in that position myself, helping out during Officers' Week, critiquing potential officers each morning. It's designed to weed out those who can't handle the pressure.

So, anyway, sure enough, our officer was chosen. He went forward and stood over Dolly, positioning her head between his legs. With a slightly unsteadily hand, I noticed, he took up the sharp knife. He said something under his breath, what it was I couldn't say, and then he slit Dolly's throat.

After the sheep was killed, we learned how to hang it up, skin it, cut it into sections and cook it in ways that would minimize our chances of being detected by enemies, avoiding tell-tale smells and smoke as much as possible. We ate stew that night, albeit feeling a bit uneasy about it.

We learned that you could eat almost anything that ran, swam or flew, as long as it was prepared and cooked properly. Name your most unappetizing animal. Rat? Sure, you can eat rat, provided it's prepared correctly. You can make rat curry. Or rat Kiev. Anything you like. The truth is, that when you're starving and haven't eaten for days, dietary qualms fade away. Meat is meat, and meat has nutrients. Besides which, it all tastes like chicken anyway.

Nor did we neglect the world of flora and fauna. A botanist joined us to point out the various mushrooms and plants that were safe to eat and how to prepare them, a skill called foraging.

Nettles, for instance, can be boiled to make a sort of tea, and although it wasn't exactly PG Tips, it provided some nutrients. Mushrooms, we were told, are trickier; most are unsafe, but we were taught to identify a few that were edible.

We were shown a series of steps to test a plant's edibility. First, separate it into its components – leaves, stems, roots, buds and flowers. Rub a small part of each component on your skin and wait for fifteen minutes to see if there's any reaction. If there's none, then place a small part of the plant on your lips, then your tongue, and finally chew a small amount without swallowing. If there's no adverse reaction after several hours, you might consider it safe to eat. Edible plants include dandelions, clovers and cattails. Clover can be eaten raw, though you might prefer boiling it to improve the taste. Plants with milky or discoloured sap, a bitter taste, a soapy texture or those that grow in swamps and stagnant water are generally best avoided.

Depending on the season, different fruits and nuts are available. In spring and summer, look for berries like strawberries, blueberries and blackberries. Not all berries are safe. Avoid white and yellow ones as they are often poisonous. If uncertain about a particular fruit, use the edibility test as above.

In the autumn, hunt for nuts such as acorns, hazelnuts and walnuts. Some nuts, like acorns, contain tannins that can make them bitter and unpalatable. To remove that, you can soak the nuts in water for several hours or boil them in several changes of water before consuming.

Most mushrooms aren't safe, so you need to be careful. The ones that are good, though, are full of nutrients, especially vitamin D and vitamin C.

'Nature provides everything we need,' said our botanist instructor. 'You just have to know where to look and what to do.'

We learned to fish using simple lines and hooks, starting out by understanding how to read a body of water and the behaviour of the fish to maximize the chances of catching one, as well as how to avoid stagnant water, which could harbour harmful bacteria. As for cooking? Boil it thoroughly and make sure it's fully cooked before you eat it.

Another important thing we covered was the survival mindset.

Finding and preparing food in the wild isn't just about technique. It's also about mindset and practicality. The search for food can be disheartening, especially when you come up empty-handed. Keeping a positive attitude and staying persistent is key. You have to remind yourself that every effort, successful or not, is a step towards survival.

Also, manage your energy. Gathering food requires energy, so always balance the effort needed with the potential reward. Avoid chasing after small animals if it's likely to expend more calories than you'll gain.

WATER

Water is as essential as rest and shelter. Without it, you die. Water is the lifeblood of our bodies, responsible for everything from regulating body temperature to lubricating joints and transporting nutrients. In a survival situation, staying hydrated is your top priority because dehydration can impair your judgment, reduce physical performance and, ultimately, threaten your life.

In the wild, it's easy to get caught up in excitement or stress and forget to drink enough water. Some signs of dehydration include dark urine, dry mouth, dizziness and fatigue. In severe cases, you might experience confusion and fainting. Monitor these signs closely and make hydration a priority. You must remind yourself to drink regularly, even when you don't feel thirsty, to keep your mind sharp, and only ever take small sips in order to conserve your supplies.

And you know what the poem says about water being everywhere but not a drop to drink? Never a truer word spoke. Therefore our lessons concentrated on how to find the most drinkable water – with fast-running streams over rocks the safest, as the movement and natural filtration reduces harmful particles – and then what to do with it when you find it.

Even if you're fairly confident that it is fresh, you have to be super-careful you don't end up drinking something that'll kill you, so the importance of purifying water was hammered into us – boiling it to kill bacteria and/or using Puritabs to make it safe to drink. We were shown how to set up a buddy system where one of us would test water (or food, come to that) first to ensure it wasn't contaminated. The idea was to wait an hour to ensure it was safe before the other consumed it.

The strategy boils down (ha ha) to this . . .

Finding it

Natural water sources

Rivers, streams, and lakes are the most obvious sources. However, these aren't always available. In dense forests or mountainous terrains, listen for the sound of running water. It can guide you even if the source is hidden. Practise the habits as described above: fast-running streams and always upstream of any animal activity.

Collecting rainwater

Rain is a fantastic source of fresh water. Use tarps, leaves and even clothing to collect rainwater. Simply spread out a tarp or some large leaves to catch rain, or if you're using clothing, wring it out into a container.

Morning dew

In the early mornings, dew can be collected from grass and leaves. It might seem tedious, but in desperate times, every drop counts. I've used cloths or absorbent materials to wipe the dew and then wring them out into a container.

Solar stills

A still is a great method for collecting water in deserts and dry climates. You dig a pit, place a container in the centre and cover the pit with a plastic sheet, which you weigh down with stones around the edges. Place a small rock in the centre of the sheet above the container. As the sun heats the ground, moisture evaporates, condenses on the plastic and drips into the container.

Vegetation

Plants can also be a water source. For example, I've cut vines and roots that ooze drinkable sap. The same goes for certain cacti and succulents, although you need to know which ones are safe. Bamboo is another plant that often holds water in its segments – not that you find much bamboo in Wales.

Purifying it

As we've said, even when you find water, it's crucial to purify it. Drinking untreated water can lead to severe illness. So . . .

Boiling

This is the most common and foolproof method. Bringing water to a rolling boil for at least one minute kills most toxins. At higher altitudes, boil for three minutes.

Filtering

If you've come prepared, you might well have a portable water filter. When not available, you can make DIY filters using layers of sand, charcoal and gravel in a container. It won't completely purify the water, but it will help to remove impurities, making it safer to boil.

Chemical purification

That is, Puritabs. Again, you're best to use them in conjunction with boiling.

NAVIGATION

The fourth-week Escape part of E&E was conducted without a compass. Prior to this, our training had always used maps and compasses. Now we would have neither. Without a compass, we had to rely on natural indicators. How?

As we learned, the sun is a reliable guide. In both hemispheres, it rises in the east and sets in the west. In the southern hemisphere, north and south swap places. Recognizing these patterns allows you to determine direction instinctively.

For instance, the side of trees covered in moss usually face north in the northern hemisphere, a small detail but crucial if you're trying to orientate yourself. We could also use the position of the sun. By observing shadows and the sun's position at different times of the day, we could determine cardinal directions. In the southern hemisphere, it's the reverse.

The wind is another vital indicator. North winds are the most common and can be identified by their effects on the environment. For example, if you see trees bending or foliage leaning in a certain direction, it's likely due to a prevailing wind. This helps in confirming your bearings.

So, for example, if I see the sun coming from a certain direction, I know immediately which way is west. If I close my eyes, get blindfolded and am taken somewhere, I just need to feel where the sun is, see the shadows, and I can figure out the directions. The sun's position, the shadows it casts, the wind direction and natural signs like tree bark and foliage all provide clues. It's about piecing together these hints to navigate accurately.

Also, we practised making a makeshift compass. By placing a needle on a leaf and floating it on a tiny drop of water, the needle would align with the Earth's magnetic field, pointing north.

So you can work out north. Knowing north is a massive help – let me give you an example. In Iraq, we knew that north was up towards Turkey, and south was down towards Saudi Arabia. So, when you're on the ground and you don't have a compass, you can still orient yourself. West is Syria and a bit southwest is Jordan. As long as you can establish north and south, you have a framework to navigate by.

Some strategy

Awareness

Always be aware of your surroundings. Notice landmarks, the position of the sun and distinctive features in the landscape. This awareness forms the foundation of good navigation.

Using the sun

The sun is a reliable guide. Again, it rises in the east and sets in the west, and by noting its position, you can roughly determine direction. At midday, the sun is generally in the south in the northern hemisphere and in the north in the southern hemisphere.

Shadow stick method

Place a stick upright in the ground and mark the tip of its shadow with a small rock or stick. Wait about fifteen minutes, then mark the tip of the shadow again. The line between the two marks runs approximately east–west, with the first mark indicating west.

Navigating by stars

As above, the stars can be your guide at night. In the northern hemisphere, find the North Star (Polaris) by locating the Big Dipper. The two stars at the end of the Big Dipper's bowl point directly to Polaris, which sits almost directly above the North Pole. In the southern hemisphere, find the Southern Cross. The longer axis of this constellation points towards the South Pole.

Using the moon

The moon can also help. If the moon rises before sunset, the illuminated side faces west. If it rises after midnight, the illuminated side faces east. This method isn't as precise as using the sun or stars, but it can give you a rough direction.

Observing nature

Nature often provides clues. As above, moss tends to grow on the north side of trees in the northern hemisphere and the south side in the southern hemisphere, though this isn't foolproof. Spider webs, ant hills and even bird flight paths can offer hints about direction.

AVOIDING CAPTURE

Top tips to evade the enemy include only moving at night, hiding up during the day and practising good camouflage and concealment drills (that old Para training coming in handy).

Mainly, though, we concentrated on dogs, which we knew would be used by the hunter force out to get us. Dogs are generally trained for specific roles. The biting dogs, like alsatians, are fearsome and made for guarding. But there's a breed, the Belgian malinois – often referred to as a skinny alsatian – that's exceptional in its resilience and fierceness, especially in enclosed spaces like buildings.

Then there are sniffer dogs, which are more often breeds like labradors or cocker spaniels, keen-nosed and relentless until they find what they're searching for. Spaniels, I learned, are particularly adept at sniffing out drugs and other contraband because of their acute sense of smell and tenacious nature.

There's this peculiar thing about how scents linger in the air, much like talcum powder. A trainer explained how, when you walk, you shed a sort of 'scent powder' which allows dogs, particularly bloodhounds, to track you. It's not actual powder, of course, but it's a useful analogy to understand how dogs can follow a trail even after the person has long gone.

To confuse the dogs, we were taught to use water and walk along a stream or river, as most dogs dislike water. Crossing a stream multiple times could also throw them off our scent.

During these training sessions, they'd bring in a dog handler, along with a padded Michelin suit that someone would volunteer to wear.

'When I say run,' the handler would instruct, 'take to your toes and I'll set the dog on you.'

As soon as the work command was given, the dog's demeanour shifted. It knew it was time to get serious. Dogs, like the harness-clad ones we trained with, become intensely focused once they know they're on the job.

The instructors teach you how to get away from the dog. For example, if you have a piece of clothing, a coat or some such, wrap it round your arm and offer it to the dog. The dog will always bite what you're offering, after which you have a number of options.

1. Get the coat off your arm and run. A lot of the time the dog will think it's still got hold of something and will keep biting on that while you make your escape.

2. Drag the dog to someplace it doesn't like. If you're near a

river, or on mud, anything that makes it difficult for that dog, get it to fix on the coat before dragging it onto some surface it doesn't like, or that will slow it down. Most dogs don't like water and will let go to swim. Or you can drown the dog.

3. Clobber the dog. While the dog is fixed on your left arm, use a weapon in your right to brain it.

We learned ways of obscuring our scent – zigzagging through rivers, staying low, moving fast. The instructors liked to remind us of scenes from old American movies with bloodhounds tracking escaped prisoners through dense swamps. Those scenes aren't just Hollywood magic; they're grounded in real tactics, though the reality is harsher. Dogs get tired, they lose interest, they need care – factors that can work in your favour.

One crucial tip shared by a dog handler stuck with me: keeping dogs happy is essential. Overwork them, or expose them to harsh conditions, and they'll lose their effectiveness.

We were always reminded that, during actual field operations, harming a service dog was strictly out of bounds. The focus was on evasion and survival, not on causing harm. These lessons weren't just about understanding how to escape. They were also about respecting the roles and lives of the animals involved, even in the most desperate situations.

The training also emphasized the importance of avoiding the local population. Farmers and locals know their land intimately and can easily spot signs of intrusion. Whether it's an imprint in the grass or disturbed foliage, they can tell when something is amiss.

Meanwhile, building a fire was about more than just warmth;

it was about staying alive. Fire could be used to cook food, purify water and signal for help. However, it also needed to be controlled to avoid detection. Cooking smells, smoke and other signs of human presence could give away our location to the enemy. We learned to minimize these signs, cooking food quickly and efficiently, and disposing of waste carefully. In the jungle, the scent of smoke or food can travel.

It's the same with our waste – as in our number twos. It all had to be bagged up and taken with us. Talking of which, one of the most surprising lessons was about how you could determine the type of troops you were up against based on their waste. For instance, British troops were known for their preference for potatoes and a penchant for meat. On the other hand, Asian troops often favoured rice and curries. By examining the waste, you could identify the race and nationality of the troops in the area.

I shit you not.

The Basics of Evasion

Stay calm
Panic can lead to poor decisions and mistakes. Take a moment to assess the situation and think through next steps calmly.

Know your pursuer
Understanding who or what you're evading is critical. Are they tracking you by sight, sound or scent? Knowing this helps tailor your evasion strategies.

Blend in

The key to successful evasion is to blend into your surroundings. You must become a part of the environment, moving silently and leaving no trace.

Stay hydrated and nourished

Staying hydrated and nourished keeps energy levels up and minds sharp.

Mental resilience

Evasion can be stressful and exhausting, so keep a positive mindset, focusing on small goals, such as reaching the next safe spot. Staying mentally resilient is as important as physical endurance.

Rest and Recovery

Finding safe spots to rest is crucial as exhaustion can lead to mistakes. Take short, strategic breaks to recharge without staying in one place too long.

Stay dry

Rather obvious. You need to maintain body heat and avoid infections. If your socks get wet, put them under your arms to dry them out.

Scavenge

We were taught to look at a discarded piece of tarpaulin not as rubbish, but as a potential lifesaving cover, or how the serrated edge of a discarded baked bean tin could become a makeshift knife. It was all about perspective, about seeing tools where others saw little. A piece of string pulled from a dustbin could be a belt or boot laces. Anything you can use as a weapon.

Have a survival kit

Meanwhile, we were introduced to rule one of Escape & Evasion: you could take only one item of survival kit. This'll be the world-famous tobacco-tin survival kit. You take an old-style tobacco tin (pretty common then, less so these days), into which you put essential items: matches, razor blades, Durex, snares, a fishing kit, needles and thread, Puritabs, a button compass and Dextrose tablets for quick energy (see the larger list below).

Our survival kit could only include the items listed above, but yours could include the following . . .

Matches These can be made waterproof by dipping the heads in melted candle wax. We also learned to start fires without modern tools, using flint and steel to create sparks. Having a flint in the box is essential.

Button compass Enough said. Don't just leave it in your kit and expect it to work. Check it's still working before you set out.

Durex The famous condom. It'll hold about two pints of water. When inserted into a sock and filled it makes it a decent canteen.

Snare Make sure you know how to use it.

Flexible saw A really good, really useful bit of kit. It'll cut much more than you think. Keep it smeared with Vaseline to stop it rusting.

Scalpel blades / razor blades You can get scalpel blades from a DIY or art-and-craft shop. Don't worry about a handle. You can make one while out in the wild. The whole idea of this kit is that it's as compact as possible and so takes up very little room in your pocket or rucksack.

Needles and thread Have a selection of needles, bearing in mind that you might want to thread it with something you find.

Tinder To pack the items and stop them from rattling. But also to help light fires, of course.

Fishhooks and line The hooks usually come in little packets. The fishing line may have a number of other uses too.

First aid kit Medical items can include plasters, suture or 'butterfly' strips, pain relief and ointment.

THE TAKEAWAY

I think this is a whole chapter of takeaways, but even so, I wanted to add that, of all the phases of Selection, it was the last one that I feared the most: Escape & Evasion. And the reason I feared it was that I had no knowledge of it, having done nothing like it before.

So let's talk about fear, again. You could have a sedentary, boring lifestyle where you never step outside your comfort zone and never feel fear. But that to me is not a life worth living. Even today, I'll have requests arrive for me to do this or that – a talk, say – and my first thought is, I can't do that. *But then the lessons kick in. I think to myself,* You don't like it. It makes you feel funny. So find out about it. Get the knowledge.

Done? Good. So now make your decision. Are you going to do it?

If you said yes, then that means commitment. It means, hard work, consistency, focus and discipline.

And if you said no? Then remember another of my favourite sayings: there are only two pains – the pain of discipline or the pain of regret. The pain of discipline won't last, and afterwards you'll be able to look at yourself in the mirror and know you tackled a challenge head-on, faced up to what frightens you and did your best regardless.

The pain of regret? That one will last forever.

CHAPTER 19

ON THE RUN

'It is a proud privilege to be a soldier – a good soldier ... [with] discipline, self-respect, pride in his unit and his country, a high sense of duty and obligation to comrades and to his superiors, and a self confidence born of demonstrated ability'

– George S. Patton Jr

At the end of the training came the final week-long exercise in Wales. We'd be taken by lorry to various drop-off points, given a sketch map and then sent on our merry way. From that point on, we'd be on the run, the goal being to put into practice everything we'd been taught in the previous three weeks.

What we had to do ...

Remain at large for a week
And while doing so ...

Survive on the bare minimum of equipment

That tobacco tin I mentioned was the only useful thing we'd be allowed to carry. Clothes-wise, we'd be wearing Second World War tackle: a heavy trench coat, old trousers (no belt – you had to sort out a belt, which invariably would be a bit of rope) and boots without laces.

Rendezvous (RV) with an agent each day

Navigating using only a sketch map (or something equally rudimentary – scribbled-down directions, say), we'd have to make our way to the RV point. We'd have a window of an hour during which the agent would wait for us. Having made contact, he would give us the location of the next RV and some food, and would also tell us if he knew anything about the movements of the enemy.

The whole RV element was based on experiences, many gleaned during the Second World War, when it was found that downed pilots, escaped POWs or troops who'd become separated from their patrol could often count on help from locals, either for humane reasons or because they were allied to a local resistance movement.

Evade the hunter force

Did I forget that bit? We'd be hunted. Our pursuers, aka the hunter force, would not know our exact location, but would have a designated area to patrol while attempting to capture us. These guys were serious about their job. It was a point of principle with them. The key was to stay ahead of them, sleeping by day and moving at night, while managing our needs for warmth, food and navigation.

What we couldn't do . . .

Miss the RV

If we failed to reach the RV during the allotted time, we wouldn't get onward instructions or food and the exercise would effectively be over. Almost certainly a fail.

Remain at large

Yes, you read that correctly. You were *not* allowed to remain at large. Capture was mandatory. So, the mind-bending thing was that we had to stay out of the clutches of the hunter force but ultimately had to allow ourselves to be captured. There was no 'escape'; we all knew how it was going to end – with interrogation. For us, it would be a matter of pride as to how long we could avoid capture. If captured earlier in the exercise, we'd be interrogated briefly and then released back into the field to continue evading. At some point, we would face the interrogation phase, whether we liked it or not.

Hurt the dogs

If you're being tracked by a dog in a real-world situation, you're best off killing the dog, and during training we'd been given strategies for doing exactly that. However, we were not allowed to harm dogs during the exercise. Nor, of course, were we allowed to harm anyone on the hunter force. Of course, this was a one-way street. They had no such qualms when it came to our well-being.

Hurt or kill livestock

Farmers take a dim view of it. Everything we'd learned regarding Dolly would have to wait until another day.

Seek help

Even though, in an actual escape scenario, seeking help from friendly civilians would be a sensible move, the exercise disallowed it. During the briefing beforehand, we were told, 'We've notified local farmers that a Selection exercise is in progress, which means there will be soldiers on their land. They've all agreed that you can be on their land. If they help you, that's up to you and up to them, but if we catch you, you'll get RTU'd. By all means, do what you have to do to get through this, but if we catch you, you fail. Got that?' I'd heard tales of blokes who had been found in a farmer's kitchen having a cup of tea. Fail. I'd heard other tales of blokes who, years later, had admitted taking help from a local. Retrospective fail and dismissal. The same went for creeping into, say, a barn or an outhouse to sleep and shelter. It wasn't strictly forbidden, but was definitely frowned upon because the farmers were letting the army use their land and nobody wants to be taking the piss.

And so the exercise began. It started with an inspection by a medic. We'd been invited to try and secrete anything useful about our persons and if the medic missed it, then good luck to us. There are various ways you can smuggle something in your body, of course. You can swallow something and then wait for it to reappear. You can put something up the other end.

I opted against. For a start, the medic was pretty thorough. I won't go into detail in case you've just had your lunch, but put it like this, he could probably see ours. As for swallowing something and retrieving it later, there was the risk of it going wrong in the field and I really didn't want to go that way. Dying in a field from an intestinal blockage? No thanks.

After the medical, we were given our kit. Well, I say kit. Webbing? Forget about it. Bergens? Yesterday's news. They'd obviously raided the Second World War dressing-up box for this gear. Out came the old and slightly mouldy overcoats, the smelly trousers and the boots that looked like they might fall apart at any second. (I was lucky; my boots stayed the course, but there were many who ended up having to make emergency repairs in the field.)

We got togged up and what a sight it was to see: we made Wurzel Gummidge look like James Bond. Later, one of the preferred modes of insult would be to call us fucking tramps. Fair enough – we did indeed look like men of the road.

You might think it was all suffering and deprivation, but in fact there was something about it I quite enjoyed. Like everybody else, I felt a great sense of trepidation, not knowing what lay ahead, only that it was going to be hard. But, at the same time, I dug the idea of having to do it all on the bones of your arse, relying on nothing but your wits and training.

There was something else I felt: a strange sense of duty to the original wearer of the trench coat. I've no idea who first wore it, of course. But I pictured him as a soldier on the frontline and I knew that whatever I was about to go through wasn't anything like what he'd had to endure.

Into a pocket of that very coat went my tobacco-tin survival kit containing matches, razor blades, Durex, snares, a fishing kit, needles and thread, Puritabs, a button compass and Dextrose tablets.

Next, we were taken in lorries to various drop-off points. Each group was handed a piece of paper with a sketch map and given a time. Be there by then.

Go.

There were three of us in my patrol: me, a bloke called Toppo and another we called Curly. The first RV made things relatively easy for us. In the biting cold and a drizzle that just wouldn't quit, we made good time and reached the location well in advance.

Standing by a tree not far away was a figure. The agent. Or was it? We had to be careful. It hardly needed stating that the hunter force could have reached the agent and replaced him with one of their own. The real bloke could have been in the back of a Land Rover, bound and gagged.

We were in plenty of time, so used the opportunity to lie in wait for a while, wary of moving forward and revealing our position right away. We were conscious of that fact that, during the day, we'd seen the Paras out and about, Land Rovers glimpsed on roads through the drizzle. We'd been skirting a field, staying in the undergrowth on the perimeter and seen some on the road close by. One of them had stopped and a couple of guys touting SLRs got out to have a piss.

Flat to the ground, Toppo, Curly and I had watched them scan the horizon looking for us, before unzipping and pissing. We'd stayed silent and still, watching them finish and go.

So now we exercised the same caution, not wanting to assume

that this guy was the genuine agent. Remember the rule? *Never assume.* It could be a trap. For that reason, only one of us went forward and only when we were as certain as we could be that he was alone.

That first night, it was me who approached the agent.

With my heart pounding, I went into a crouched run. He saw me coming and tensed. I stopped some distance away, feeling exposed, ready to dive to one side if he suddenly produced a weapon. The hunter teams were allowed to open fire on us. They'd be using blanks, of course, but even so.

'It's quite grey tonight,' I said.

'Yes, but we're expecting blue skies tomorrow.'

With our respective bona fides established, I called Toppo and Curly forward and they emerged from the night like a couple of watchful rural hobos, cautious but looking forward to whatever food the agent might have for us. Handed to us in a hessian sack, it was profoundly disappointing. It soon became a running joke that 'food' in the context of Escape & Evasion meant turnips and maybe potatoes and carrots if we were lucky. Evidently, our agents were unable to lay their hands on KitKats or Lion bars. The only things they were able to give us were items that needed cooking. Okay, fair enough, carrots don't need cooking, but everything else required preparation. Boiling, of course.

This presented us with a problem. Firstly, we would need to devote time to building our fire, finding water and boiling our turnips. Secondly, we ran the risk that our fire would give away our location. It was a conversation we'd have several times over the next five days. We'd also discuss trying to identify rabbit runs and catch something to cook. Same problem. Also, time was always the issue. I'm not saying that we neglected our training. It was just that the need to outwit the hunters and reach the next RV was paramount. Everything else shuttled into second place. Besides, you have to be careful what you eat because it can often stress the body to digest it. Guess which vegetables are particularly difficult to digest? Cruciferous ones, including turnips.

Next, the agent showed us a map, told us where we needed to be and gave us a window in which we needed to be there. 'Your agent will only be there for an hour,' we were told. 'Don't be late.'

Yeah, thanks. We knew that.

Having memorized the RV location, we set off, using the remaining hours of darkness to get as far as we could. In the distance, we saw headlights strobe the night sky. Perhaps they were from the hunter team, or maybe just a member of the public. It didn't matter. They were far enough away that they weren't an issue. What's more, it had stopped raining at last.

Now, as the day began to make its presence felt, and the silhouettes of trees and the skyline gained more shape, we decided to stop and rest up. Found a hedgerow. Lay down. Went to sleep.

Waking up, I realized that we hadn't chosen our rest stop nearly as carefully as we'd thought. In fact, we were quite exposed. I could hear traffic. Next, I saw a Land Rover pass by and realized it belonged to the enemy. It stopped some 50 metres away and out poured a load of Paras complete with tracker dogs. We heard them chatting. Dogs snuffling, barking.

Between ourselves, we whispered, trying to decide. *Do we make a run for it? Have they seen us or is it just coincidence? Are they having a brew break? A toilet break? Letting the dogs relieve themselves? Or are they getting orientated?*

What the Paras tended to do was drop off a patrol, let them hunt on foot and then return a few hours later to pick them up.

One good rule of thumb was that if you had to assume (and you should never assume), you should assume the worst. Thus, we were getting ready to make our move and take ourselves out of the scent range for the dogs when suddenly they all piled back into the Land Rover and it was panic over.

The day was tense. We stayed hidden in hedgerows, snoozed, shivered and munched on carrots. We had a sentry system, stagging on to keep watch for signs of the enemy, waiting for it to get dark so we could set off. Our next RV was at 1 a.m.

That night, we arrived at the RV, a junction of two tracks, well over an hour before the allotted time, which suited us fine. We mounted what we call a listening watch, where we stayed out of sight and totally hidden, listening and watching, trying to detect any sound or movement, any activity.

We kept an eye on the animals in the field, especially the sheep. It's especially useful to keep an eye on the sheep; they notice everything. Sitting there quietly for hours, we saw all sorts of wildlife – foxes, badgers, mice, voles, weasels. When you sit there silent and still, they get used to you. You're just another part of the ecosystem.

Eventually, we saw a lone figure approach the junction. We didn't come out of hiding just yet. There was a building not far away and we'd been watching it carefully, having worked out that if the hunter force were monitoring the RV, that's where they would hide.

When we did eventually speak to him, the guy was jittery – maybe pretending to be for the purposes of the exercise. He handed us a sack which later turned out to contain potatoes. 'Are you okay?' he asked. 'You look cold.'

We were indeed very cold. Toppo had scavenged a fertilizer bag that he'd used to try to insulate himself, but it had crackled so much that we made him get rid of it.

We were also very tired and when we left the agent that night, making our way to the treeline with the black night already turning to grey, we were all thinking about getting some rest. It's not optional in a situation like that. Getting rested is as important as getting nutrition. Without it, you're impaired, not just physically but mentally, too.

We tabbed for a few miles, trying to make good time before the light made it too risky to move. Moving through a spinney with the undergrowth tearing at our clothes, Curly spotted a building in the near-distance and we made our way to it. It was a barn, open at both ends, used to house a tractor as well as various bits of agricultural equipment I couldn't put a name to.

'We could go in there,' he suggested.

The idea was tempting. The chances were that there'd be somewhere in there to lay our heads, maybe even some bits and pieces we could scavenge. I still needed a belt for my trousers. Something gave me pause for thought, though. I don't know what it was. Some kind of sixth sense maybe, and in a very low voice, I told Toppo and Curly to stop. *Wait. Just indulge me.*

Sure enough, we'd been there about ten minutes when we saw movement. In the doorway of the barn, we caught the silhouette of a soldier who moved quickly. A moment later, we heard the unmistakable pitter-patter sound of a Para taking a leak. Call me a genius, but they'd been in there waiting for us. Of course. A tempting-looking building like that. A passing team was bound to be attracted to it. We left them to it.

The following day, a farmer almost discovered us. He drove his tractor with a water bowser attached, heading straight towards our hiding spot. Had he seen us? He stopped 20 feet away, got out and lit a cigarette. A sheepdog appeared, sniffing around, adding to our anxiety. We remained still, hoping he wouldn't investigate. Then we heard his wife, calling to him or maybe to the dog. After what felt like an eternity, he got back in his tractor and drove away.

Maybe he knew we were there but was sticking to the agreement. Maybe he didn't. Either way, we decided to move to a different location. He hadn't helped or hindered us, but what if he did know we were there? After all, farmers have a sixth sense regarding their land. And what if he then got chatting to the hunter force who bribed him with more cigarettes? From the head shed, we'd learned that there were plenty of farmers who didn't like us hanging around in their fields and would be more than happy to put a spanner in the works.

We couldn't risk it. So even though it was daylight, we decided to move on, but kept to the hedgerows, eventually finding a new spot to lie low. We continued our routine: stagging on, eating, resting and drinking water purified with Puritabs. For sustenance, we ate the carrots given to us by the agents.

Helicopters would pass overhead. Were they for us? We weren't sure. But although it was sensible to assume a worst-case scenario, one thing I would say about helicopters is that they're pretty shit for surveillance purposes. You need to know roughly where someone is before they're any use. They sound scary but aren't much cop for hunting people on foot. Not unless you know where they are.

The cold saps your energy. We knew that. And we knew to take care when it came to rest and food. During the daylight hours, sleep might not come, but we tried to remember that rest is vital. We would stay still in the undergrowth, watching the wildlife around us, knowing its presence was a good sign. On one occasion, a Land Rover passed not far away and the various animals reacted a good thirty seconds or so before we heard it.

On the afternoon of the third day, Curly and Toppo were napping while I kept watch and I heard the sound of engines. Waking up, we saw two Land Rovers speeding down the road. They stopped and a group of Paras jumped out, running towards a hedgerow. They seemed to have seen something, were moving purposefully and checking the hedges thoroughly. And then they left.

It had started to rain – as in, really pour down. We went from being very cold to very cold and very wet. Our clothes were soaked through, those heavy trench coats like lead weights.

You know what we didn't do, though? We didn't complain and bitch and moan. We just got on with it. We stayed vigilant and alert. We remembered our training.

It was the fourth day by now and we were exhausted. However, we had evaded capture, which was a massive boost. What we knew was that if you were captured before the end of the Escape & Evasion phase (in other words, before the five- to seven-day window), you would be interrogated for up to twelve hours and then sent back into the field to continue the exercise. We'd all agreed that it sounded like just about the most demoralizing outcome possible.

I figured that if we could survive day five, we should be okay. We were cold, starving, half-dead from fatigue. But if we could just get through day five . . .

So, it came to day five, early that morning, maybe 1 a.m. or 2 a.m., and we were approaching the RV point slowly as planned. We had to climb over a fence and edge down a field. Leading the way, I saw sheep ahead suddenly moving quickly, as though they were being parted by an invisible force.

And right away, I was like, *Uh-oh. This ain't right.*

At the same time, I heard the distinct thud of people running.

My instincts screamed ambush and I bolted, sprinting through the sheep, which scattered in all directions. Toppo and Curly did the same, disappearing into the murk of the night. As I ran, I could hear voices closing in. 'Right. Come up on the right!' someone shouted. Multiple pursuers, I knew, were descending on me from all directions.

The next thing I knew, an almighty tackle took me down and I hit the cold ground hard. I immediately tried to get to my feet but was unable to do so because there were at least three guys on top of me, effing and jeffing, screaming at me to lay down and stay still, and making their point with fists and feet.

'Stay where you are. Stay down.'

They punched and kicked, ensuring I remained on the deck. Only when they were satisfied that I posed no threat did they yank me up by the scruff of my neck. Summoning a burst of strength, I fought back, trying to break free, but there were too many of them and they wrestled me to the ground again, resuming the beating. These were Paras. Hard blokes. They knew how to take it and they knew how to dish it out.

I could hear more shouting from not far away and vaguely wondered about the fate of Toppo and Curly. Toppo hadn't been as conscientious about hygiene as me and Curly and had developed some kind of rash on his undercarriage. Even walking was painful for him, let alone running. I didn't fancy his chances. Anyway, I had other things to worry about, namely Des Powell and whether the Paras would get too carried away. These were guys who let their fists do the talking. And their fists were very insistent.

They dragged me across the field. We reached a barbed-wire fence. Tenderly, the Paras passed me over so as to make sure I didn't get snagged. I'm joking. It was the opposite of that. I was spiked by metal as they shoved me over, practically using me as a means of protecting themselves from the metal spikes.

For a second, they struggled and I thought I had a chance, landing in a painful heap on the other side of the fence and preparing to make a run for it. No such luck. There were more of the Maroon Machine on the other side. They scraped me off the mud, screaming at me as they hoiked me up by the armpits and dragged me up a steep hill towards where I knew there was a road.

Vehicle lights. A Land Rover. They let me drop to my knees so that I was now in front of the headlights, breathless and disoriented.

A Para came right in my face, spitting and shouting, 'Get your fucking clothes off now!'

I did nothing.

'You've got thirty seconds to strip!'

They yanked me to my feet, but stayed close, ready to pounce if I tried anything. I started to undress, fumbling with my coat, which was tied with rope that I had (at last) scavenged during the exercise. They grew impatient, tugging at my clothes until, finally, I managed to shed my coat, then my shirt and trousers, which again were held up by makeshift belts of string and wire.

Standing there naked, I shivered uncontrollably in the cold, early-morning air. The rain had soaked everything and the wet ground only added to the chill. They left me standing there, exposed and vulnerable, shivering in the cold, and mocked me – 'What the fuck's this? You're a fucking tramp!' – until, after what felt like an eternity, they ordered me to put my clothes back on, giving me another thirty seconds. As I scrambled to dress, they shouted at me to hurry, all the while trying to keep me off-balance and disoriented, hardly letting me finish dressing before they laid into me again, knocking me to the deck, lashing out as I curled up into a protective ball, doing anything I could to try to minimize the pain.

Thank God they decided that enough was enough, and they hauled me up and threw me into the Land Rover. For the first time, I saw that they were wearing cam cream.

Once inside the vehicle, they shoved me down and, with boots on the back of my head, forced my face against the cold metal floor. My body ached from the beatings, my mind reeling from the intensity of the capture, each bump of the road sending jolts of pain through my battered body. I focused on the basics, reminding myself to keep breathing, to stay conscious.

The thing was, I knew that worse was ahead.

THE TAKEAWAY

Escape & Evasion felt like a situation in which I wasn't in control. I had anxiety about that. To overcome it, I went back to the basics. I looked to the things I knew I could control – warmth, shelter, navigation, observation – and I made sure to do those things well.

At the same time, I told myself not to worry about the things I couldn't control. You control what you know you are in control of. The rest of it is in the lap of the gods. By focusing on those uncontrollable elements, you'll neglect the basics, which in turn reduces your chances of success.

CHAPTER 20

BOY IN THE HOOD

'I am the master of my fate; I am the captain of my soul'
– William Ernest Henley

The back of an Army Land Rover, like every other bit of an Army Land Rover, is designed for efficiency, not comfort. I ended up on the floor in the middle, with my tormentors' boots pressing down on me, which is a pretty good metaphor for the situation I found myself in.

What's that horror film? *Keep telling yourself it's only a movie.* Me, I had to keep telling myself it was only an exercise. It's as real-world as they can make it, but it was never going to get as bad as the real thing.

Was it?

The doors slammed shut. The engine roared to life. I tried to lift my head, to get a glimpse of my surroundings, anything, but a voice barked at me to keep my head down. Any time I dared move, they kicked or jabbed me back into submission, so fuck that for a game of soldiers, to coin a phrase.

The Land Rover picked up speed. No one spoke, apart from the occasional order for me to keep still or, when they booted me and I cried out in pain, to tell me to shut up. The journey couldn't have taken more than twenty minutes, though felt like an eternity. Finally, the vehicle lurched to a stop and they dragged me out.

Back on solid ground at last, I caught a glimpse of our surroundings. I saw fences – proper wooden ones, not wire – and a few buildings coming into view. I saw a dark and rundown farmhouse building and, to the left of it, what looked like a small warehouse, a building that seemed to squat there, awaiting its prey.

It must have been around 3 a.m. by now. Most of the world was safely tucked up in bed as yours truly was dragged towards a door at the front of the warehouse. A cage-lamp above the door illuminated chipped metalwork.

They called the warehouse the Pen. We hadn't been told about it, not officially – just that after Escape & Evasion came Resistance to Interrogation – but rumours had swirled around the group, so I was pretty sure I knew what lay in store. Either way, I knew that the Pen was to be my home for the foreseeable.

I expected them to drag me direct to the door, but they didn't. Instead, I was shoved to my knees. A hand grabbed my hair and pulled at it so that I had no choice to but to look at the warehouse. The meaning was obvious. *Look at it. Look what we're about to do with you.*

And even though it was just a phase of Selection and not real-world, and even though it was a corny trick designed to scare me, I don't mind admitting that it worked. Kneeling there, the warehouse with its one blazing eye in front of me, I was terrified.

'We hope you'll be happy in your new home,' growled a mocking voice from behind me.

And then something else happened. A second voice said 'Wait, wait.' Hands were removed from my shoulders and the two guys moved in front of me, one of them crouching down to talk to me.

'Look, mate,' he said. 'I'm Para, you're Para. I'm gonna do you a solid.' He waved his hand. 'Go on. Take to your toes. We'll say you gave us the slip.'

I was tempted.

I mean, don't get me wrong. It wasn't as though I took him at his word. The smirk he wore told me as much. But one thing we'd been taught was that, in the event of capture, you should try to escape as early as you can, before you become too brutalized to even try. And they had temporarily released me. I saw me throwing myself back, using one hand to pivot then sweeping their legs from under them with my feet. By the time they were back upright, I'd be gone, maybe with one of their SLRs under my arm. What a story that would be.

But no. Capture, remember, was mandatory. The interrogation phase was compulsory. This was just a couple of Para guys trying to mess with my head and nearly succeeding. Fuck them.

I stayed on my knees and watched as they laughed and gave each other high-fives. Pair of twats.

One of them stepped behind me. I sensed him bend down. The next thing I knew, a bag was pulled over my head and my world went to black.

As far as I can tell, the standard of hoods has improved since back then. They're black these days, and although I don't know what fabric they use, it doesn't look too abrasive.

This hood, on the other hand, was a hessian sack, exactly like the turnip bags. Scratchy? Don't get me started. It wasn't so much hood as exfoliant. And it had an incredible ability to retain moisture.

Its only benefit was that I could see enough to register light change, and to even detect movement if it happened right in front of you. It also allowed me to see just underneath it, which wasn't much practical use unless I fancied conducting a study of people's boots, but did at least give me a little psychological boost. It meant that while I was cut off, I wasn't *completely* cut off.

I was hauled up by my two laughing pals and dragged forward. I could make out the light above the warehouse door. It grew bright as we approached. My breathing increased. I was panting, the hessian pressed to my lips, as I heard the door dragged open and I was bundled inside.

It was cold in the Pen. Just as cold as outside, as far as I could tell. But where the air outside was fresh and had a snap, the atmosphere in the Pen was dank, damp and clammy. It was foetid air, rank with foreboding.

I could hear noise from somewhere within the building, a distant clamour like that of a prison. Through the slit at the bottom of my hood, I saw dirty, grey-painted concrete flooring and breeze blocks for walls. From somewhere, a shout of pain cut through the sound of my captors' boots on an unforgiving concrete floor. At the same time, I tried to keep track of our progress – counting steps and turns as we continued along corridors – but lost count. I became aware of a noise, a constantly droning *shshsh* sound that seemed to be getting louder, as though we were approaching the source.

We were. Finally, they bundled me into a room and I knew that, wherever I was, I had arrived.

If pain has a smell, this room smelled of it. A fusty, damp, evil odour. Any sound was drowned out by the constant *shshsh* sound of white noise, the relentless hiss of an out-of-tune radio. The noise was loud, punishing. A sound designed to disorient and unsettle.

I was shoved up against a wall. They roughly used their boots to kick my feet into position and placed my forearms on the wall so that I was leaning forward.

'Not a word,' said one of them. 'Feel this?'

Something – maybe a fist, maybe a rifle barrel – smashed into my temple and I cried out in pain.

It came again. Warm blood trickled down the side of my face.

'I said not a word. Now stay where you are. Exactly as you are.' He had moved his face so that it was close to my ear. '*Exactly* as you are.'

I was now in what's known as a stress position, a standing or sitting posture that places weight on various muscle groups. For one of them, you just squat and hold, which makes your thigh muscles burn like you can't believe. A second involves adopting a seated position with your back against the wall, legs at right angles, as though sitting on an invisible chair. At first, it doesn't seem so bad, but after only a short time, you gradually become aware of the discomfort and the fact that you can do nothing to alleviate it. Try to move? *Smash* comes a fist or rifle. Fall to the floor? Same.

And that was how they left me.

I wouldn't say the pain set in quickly. That's the thing about a stress position. At first you think, *This ain't so bad. I can deal with this.* And then it dawns on you that you can't move even if you want to, which itself is a form of psychological torture. Then the muscles very gradually start to overload. You begin to tremble. The pain starts to creep up on you. You'll do anything for it to end. Want to know how to stop time? Get in a stress position. I tried to count the seconds, the minutes, anything to keep my mind focused. They'd warned us about this, impressing on us the need to endure, to keep our minds sharp even when our bodies were failing. Even so, it never got easier to bear. I never found a way to overcome or master the pain.

The white noise enveloped me, masking all other sound, although occasionally something would break through. Shouting. Moaning. Was that a scream? Every so often, a guard would adjust my position, straightening my arms, pressing a knee into my back to keep me upright. My body ached and my mind teetered on the edge of exhaustion, but I had to hold on. The constant noise, the cold concrete floor, the oppressive darkness under the hood – it all blurred together into a single, unending trial.

They lifted me suddenly, the abrupt change in position a jarring shock. I stumbled as they dragged me to another part of the room, pushing me into yet another stress position.

I was moved again. Another seated position. Legs bent. Muscles crying out in agony. *The body's not supposed to do this*, I kept thinking. *It's not supposed to do this.*

I risked a movement, turned my head and could see another pair of feet beside me. Someone else was in the room, enduring the same torment. It was a small comfort, knowing I wasn't alone in this. The thought that others were being put through the same ordeal somehow made it more bearable.

Time dragged on. Minutes felt like hours, with each second a battle against my own body and mind. This was the resistance to interrogation phase, I reminded myself, which meant the interrogation bit was yet to come.

Something we'd been taught was to try to keep track of time. The main way of doing this was to count, being sure to note anything that appeared to be happening on a regular basis. Here, I relied on the rhythm of my captors' actions. I counted one-one-thousand, two-one-thousand, and worked out that, every twenty to thirty minutes, they were moving me into a different stress position.

Each time they did so, it felt like relief – even though different muscles would soon be shrieking in agony. I was grateful for some evidence that they clearly didn't intend to push me to the brink of collapse; they needed me coherent enough to undergo interrogation.

Through the blanket of white noise, I could hear the door open and close. I tried to mind-map the room based on the faintest clues – footsteps, shuffling movements, the occasional murmur. I was pretty sure that people entered and some left. Were these other prisoners, or guards? As I mentioned before, we'd been taught that, if you planned to try to escape, do it as close to the start of your captivity as you can – when you still have your strength, when you still have your marbles.

Stress position standing, stress position sitting – no breaks in between. Three cycles per hour, roughly.

Then, after what felt like an eternity, hands lifted me roughly and I was hauled from the room, feet dragging as we moved. As we left the room, something fundamental changed and it took me a second or two to work out what it was. The white noise. *There was no white noise.* A feeling of euphoria washed over me, so intense it was almost worth the pain just to feel that release from it. My muscles were no longer in agony. My senses were released from captivity.

As I was lugged down a corridor, I tried to map the building, coming to the conclusion that I was being taken deeper into the complex. I could hear shouting in the distance. Was it the sound of someone being duffed up? I wasn't sure. More shouting.

Suddenly, we stopped. A door opened and I was pulled into a room filled with warmth, a stark contrast to the cold I had grown accustomed to in the white-noise room. With hands on my shoulders, they sat me down roughly. I felt the hard, uncomfortable surface of an old wooden chair beneath me.

And the hood was removed.

Another of my senses freed and returned to me.

Again, the relief.

I blinked against the sudden brightness. A single lightbulb swung above me, casting harsh shadows in what was a small, whitewashed room. Across from me sat a bloke in civvy clothes – parka, blue jeans and mountain boots. He was clean-shaven, his appearance non-descript, almost mundane. Between him and me was a small table. On it, a notebook, a pen, a flask of tea and a pack of cigarettes.

'Hello, Des. How are you?' he asked. His voice was pleasant, almost kindly.

I blinked at him.

'My name's Tom, by the way,' he smiled. 'It's good to meet you.'
I said nothing.

'You must be cream-crackered, mate. Been a long haul for you, hasn't it?'

Having been kept the way I had, I wanted to talk. I'm a garrulous bloke and I longed to hear my own voice just to check that I was still alive.

I bit down on any response, said nothing, because the one thing I knew of interrogation was what I'd had drilled into me during training. I was only to give my name, rank, number and date of birth. Anything more could be manipulated, used against me. A simple yes or no could be edited into a tape. For the same reason, you can't nod or shake your head.

'Come on, let's hear it. Are you okay? How's your body? Do you need any medical attention?' His questions were disarming.

I coughed, which was partly because I needed to cough and partly because I wanted to come across more afflicted than I really was. It's a tactic designed to try and play on your captors' sympathies. You allow them to think you're at a low ebb so they'll go easy on you or give you food and drink.

I maintained my silence, trying to project a demeanour of exhaustion over and above what I actually felt. At the same time, my eyes were adjusting to the light, scanning the room for any clues, any advantages. A heater hummed nearby, its comforting sound in stark contrast to the aural filth of the white-noise room.

'Tell you what, you probably don't feel like talking just yet,' said Tom, across the table. 'How about instead you have some coffee?' He poured a steaming cup from the flask. God, it smelled good.

Without hesitation, I reached for the cup and, although the coffee was almost scalding, sipped it gratefully.

Another thing we're taught: if you're offered food and drink, take it. Yes, there is the very small risk it's poisoned or drugged. But if they really wanted to drug you, there are a million other ways. Chances are they want to soften you up.

He watched me drink approvingly, an almost fatherly look in his eyes, before going on to talk, his tone casual. 'Look, Des, we know you're SAS. Let's cut to the chase, shall we? What have you been doing? Who's on Selection with you?'

My mind went back to what we'd been taught about coping in situations like this.

For a start, I knew the interrogation was designed to simulate an aspect of capture known as TQ, 'tactical questioning'. It therefore had two aims.

1. To destroy captives' spirit, but without harming you beyond repair, or you'd be no good for . . .

2. . . . the questioning, which is for a local commander to assess whether you're needed (that is, useful) for further questioning at a more advanced facility.

What else did I know?

That you should be the 'grey man', neither submissive nor aggressive. You must stare straight ahead if you can, in order that your eye movements don't give anything away. They might bring in one of your team members, for example, and looks between you could somehow alert your captors. A glance up and to the left is thought to mean that you're telling the truth. A look up and to the right is supposed to mean that you're lying.

Something else: under the Geneva Convention, you only have

to give those four details – the big four, they call them: name, rank, number and date of birth.

And so, my reply to Tom was, 'Powell. Corporal. 2-4-4-4-4-7-5-5. 26.10.1956.'

His demeanour didn't slip, not one bit. 'Come on, Des. This is getting a bit real, isn't it?'

I thought about it later, the way he used that particular phrase, the precise wording of which was surely a means of exploiting doubt that festered in the minds of all the exhausted, sensory-deprived captives. This is just an exercise, right? Just an exercise.

Keep telling yourself it's only a movie.

'Come on, Des. We can let your family know you're okay.'

Again, his words introduced doubt. Was I really on Selection or was this something else entirely? The line between training and reality blurred, and I struggled to maintain my composure. The room's warmth, the coffee, the casual conversation – all of it was designed to disarm me, to make me question everything.

I gave him nothing but the basics. 'Powell,' I said. 'Corporal. 2-4-4-4-4-7-5-5. 26.10.1956.'

My voice was slow, deliberate.

He sighed, putting down his cup.

'Guard,' he called out. The door burst open. The hood went back over my head and rough hands hoisted me from the chair. The coffee spilled as I was dragged back down the corridor, heels scraping the floor.

Back into the white-noise room I went, where the cold and the harsh concrete was a stark contrast to the brief warmth of the interrogation room.

They put me back into the stress position, the standing one.

The smell of the hood was familiar, though you wouldn't call it comforting, and it was still slightly damp around the mouth area. When I breathed in, I sucked it to my mouth and the hessian tickled my lips. The wall beneath my hands felt rough and cold.

Time passed. The cycle began again. I counted. Twenty minutes multiplied by sixty seconds. When I got to a count of 1,200 and nobody came, it was almost a worse torture than the torture itself. No doubt they did it deliberately to mess with our heads.

The way everything in the Pen was designed to mess with your head.

Occasionally, a guard would lift my hood and offer me a sip of water, just enough to keep me from dehydration. Nothing was said, but the water was like nectar.

Hallucinations began to creep in – snatches of music, imagined signals. After a while, it became so I wasn't sure what was real anymore.

One thousand, two hundred.

The guards' adjustments kept me from collapsing completely. I thought back to my counting from last time. Two hours, I guessed, before they came to fetch me for the next interrogation. Interrogation was a welcome respite from the white noise and stress positions. What I really needed, though, was sleep.

Gradually, I became more aware of the other guys in the room. I wondered if Curly and Toppo were in there with me. Through the gap in my hood, I saw a foot on the floor beside mine and, as I watched, it came across to give my boot a tap. A comforting tap.

That was Toppo, I decided. I remember that boot. I should do: I'd watched him hold it aloft to empty out the dirt and grit enough times. As it came across to touch mine, I felt a little surge of elation and hope, a feeling that I was no longer so alone.

When I get out of this, I thought to myself, *I'm gonna give that lad the biggest hug.*

(But you know what? When I did eventually get out and I spoke to Toppo, I found out it wasn't him who tapped my foot. When we compared notes, we came to the conclusion that we hadn't even been in the same room at the same time. Weird.)

It was during this when they came for me again. Hands pulled me to my feet, spun me around and led me out of the room and down the corridor. Through the hessian, light changed. Once more, the release from the white noise was blissful.

This time, however, the journey felt different. I sensed a longer walk, a different turn, before being seated once more. Again, the warmth in the room was a contrast to the cold of the noise room. I felt more pairs of hands steady me and sensed there were more people here than before.

The hood was yanked off, taking half my face with it.

I blinked against the light, struggling to adjust.

On the table were half-eaten sandwiches, a flask and biscuits on the table. The heater hummed nearby, adding to the stifling warmth. Looking up, there were two interrogators. One stood with his knuckles on the tabletop, King Kong-style. His face was red, like he'd just had an exasperating interaction with a call centre. There was another guy who lounged in a corner with his hands in his pockets.

'Name?' barked Redface. No introductions this time. No Tom with his offer of coffee and pleasant bedside manner. Just Redface and the Cornerstone, who seemed to take a detached interest in proceedings. I'd have to watch that one, I thought. If Redface was the bad cop, he'd be the good one.

(Incidentally, me calling him Redface is/was a deliberate tactic. One technique we were taught as captives is to pick on some aspect of an interrogator and use it to mentally undermine him. You never say anything, of course – you're the grey man, remember. It's just a mental game you play with yourself, one that helps you feel higher status than your captors and keeps you alert.)

I responded mechanically, 'Powell,' I said. 'Corporal. 2-4-4-4-4-7-5-5. 26.10.1956.'

A mantra to cling to.

'I didn't ask you for your rank and number, numb-nuts. And I sure as fuck aren't going to send you a birthday card, so I don't need your date of birth either. Now, shall we start again? *Name.*'

'Powell,' I said. 'Corporal. 2-4-4-4-4-7-5-5. 26.10.1956.'

The man leaned in, his face inches from mine. 'You think you're nails, do you?' he spat. 'We know you're SAS. What's your name?' he demanded again.

'Powell,' I said. 'Corporal. 2-4-4-4-4-7-5-5. 26.10.1956.'

His colour deepened. He threw a look at Cornerstone whose eyebrows raised a fraction.

'You know, don't you, that we'll put you back in the room?'

I said nothing.

Cornerstone spoke up. 'See sense, Des,' he said, coming on like Tom's kindlier brother. 'We don't want to put you back there. You don't want to go back there. You want to be out here with us, having a sarnie and a cup of tea.'

I did the big four.

Redface thrust himself forward. His eyes bore into mine, trying to break my resolve. 'I know a northern tosspot when I see one. Sheffield isn't it, Powell? Now, tell us why you're here. We know you're not alone. Start by giving us the names of your patrol.'

Big four.

Redface lost it. From the table, he picked up an open can of Fanta and threw it at the wall. It left a smear and hit the concrete with a wet clunk. I jumped a little as he did so, cursed myself for letting anything show, even that.

And now Cornerstone, perhaps sensing that I'd been softened a little, pushed himself off the wall and came close to the table. 'Come on, give us something. Just give us a little titbit. A name. Fred or Bill.'

Big four.

Redface and Cornerstone looked at each other. Cornerstone sighed, lifted his hand and gave me a little wave goodbye. I met his gaze as the dreaded hood came back over my head and I cried out in surprise as I was grabbed from behind.

Back to the room.

(When was the last time I slept?)

Back into the stress position.

(Years ago, it felt like.)

Was it that time that I yelled in pain and got another clout for my troubles? I wasn't sure. I do think it was that time I started to hear the music, though. It was a piece of classical music that I recognized from an advert on the television. A cigar advert, wasn't it? I found it quite soothing, spacey. I felt light and heady, like a kid drinking his first pint of snakebite.

'Des,' whispered a voice. Was it Toppo? Curly, maybe? Another bloke from a different patrol.

I said nothing.

'Des, can you hear me?' I didn't recognize the voice, but it seemed to be coming from right beside me. I looked for feet and saw none. 'Des, can you hear me?' he repeated.

Before, I'd got clobbered just for gasping in pain. No way was I going to speak.

'Des, have you told them anything? I told them a few things, just to keep them interested. In return they gave me biscuits. Squashed-fly biscuits. Custard creams and bourbons. I split the bourbon open and licked off the chocolate filling, just like I used to when I was a kid. Best biscuit I've ever had, Des, I'm telling you.'

'Are you real?' I wanted to say. 'Am I imagining you? Either way, could you put a sock in it? I'm trying to get tortured here.'

But I kept quiet.

And counted.

And sipped the water gratefully when it was brought, like a bee on a flower. A beautiful bee on a fragrant flower. That was me.

Until they came for me again.

They dragged me from the room, along the corridor and into the interrogation room where I was seated once more. The hood was removed. The warmth and light were almost blinding after the darkness. A new interrogator sat before me, his demeanour calm and sincere.

No, he wasn't new. It was Tom. Or was it? Maybe it was Cornerstone?

Were Cornerstone and Tom one and the same?

It suddenly struck me that the voice back in the white-noise room could have been Tom, or maybe Cornerstone. Were they trying to trick me?

'Des, are you okay?' said Tom-who-might-be-Cornerstone, his tone gentle. 'We've noticed some guys aren't feeling well. What about you? Are you all right? You've got a nasty cut on the side of your head there. Did one of our lads get a bit over-enthusiastic?'

I stayed silent.

'Look, you need to let us know you're okay. How about you nod your head?'

I remained still.

'Okay, then, blink.'

I did nothing.

'There we go,' he smiled. 'We got a blink. You *are* okay.'

God, you sneaky bastard, I wanted to shriek, but of course stayed silent.

'Well, good, we're making progress at last,' he said. 'Tea?'

He looked at me, waiting in vain for a response, and then shook his head in mock frustration, pouring me one anyway. 'Now, it turns out that we're not the only ones worried about you. Your family have been in touch with the Regiment. Apparently, your mother's worried sick that she hasn't heard from you in a while, so we need to send a message through the Red Cross.' He stifled a yawn. 'It's just a formality really. Can you sign this?'

On the table was a piece of paper, which he pushed towards me.

'Oh, pen,' he pretended to remember, fished one from his hoodie and slid over a Bic biro. I reached for the tea, sipping it slowly, savouring the warmth. Without being asked, I took a biscuit. It was a bourbon. Or was it? I was no longer sure. I bit into it, hoping that it was indeed a biscuit.

'Just sign it, Des. It'll let your family know you're okay,' he urged, his eyes sincere.

I shook my head, repeating my script. 'Powell,' I said. 'Corporal. 2-4-4-4-4-7-5-5. 26.10.1956.'

He sighed, leaning back. 'I know they've told you not to sign anything, but think about it. Your family is worried. We can get you a proper meal, some rest. Just sign it.'

I remained silent, my resolve hardening. He continued to press, his words blurring into the background as I focused on the tea and biscuits. It was a small victory, but one I clung to.

Eventually, he gave up. 'You might regret this,' he said, his tone shifting to one of threat. 'Guard!' he called out.

The bag was placed over my head again and I was dragged back to the pen, where the cycle resumed: the stress positions, the cold, the white noise. My mind drifted, plagued by exhaustion. I saw faces, heard voices and wondered if they were real.

In the midst of this, I began to doubt. Was this really part of Selection? Or was it something more? The interrogators had planted seeds of uncertainty. Were we being prepared for something else? A different phase of training? The paranoia grew, feeding on my exhaustion like a hungry dog on a tasty bone.

But I held on. This was a battle, I knew. It was a battle of wills and I intended to win.

Hands grasped me, ripped me to my feet and took me to the interrogation room for what I thought was probably interrogation number four. And if each one was different, they'd really flipped the script for this one.

THE TAKEAWAY

The interrogation represented a step into the unknown, but it wasn't as if anything came as a surprise. Even so, it was hard and to get through it I asked myself this question: How much do I want this?

I'll tell you. I'd been through training with the Paras and then Selection with SAS, and the answer was that I wanted it more than anything. Now, I could talk all day (and have) about hard work, consistency, focus and discipline, but sometimes what you're doing transcends even that. Sometimes you simply need to draw on spirit and grit. And in the Des Powell Top Trumps game, those are the two highest-scoring cards. Spirit and grit. There is no substitute for those qualities.

CHAPTER 21

THE LIGHT AT THE END OF THE TUNNEL

'The summits are our own on these hills we choose to climb. We are the creators of the future, we are the conquerors sublime'

– Jean Arno

It was a woman.

The interrogator this time around was a woman.

I had clocked that there were two people waiting in the interrogation room. I could see silhouettes through the hessian hood, but only became aware that the interrogator was female when they took off the hood.

And there's no getting around it – she was a beautiful woman. I have no idea if she was chosen for her looks or for her attitude, but both, it turned out, were ideal for the job.

I wasn't shocked, though. Any surprise comes in thinking back, because at the time I was just a shell. A brittle, exhausted husk of a person. The Queen could have been standing there talking to Lord Lucan and I wouldn't have turned a hair.

The woman, blonde hair in a ponytail, wore a khaki jumpsuit and she looked at me with a mixture of impatience and disdain.

'Ah, Mr Powell,' she said, her tone dripping with sarcasm. 'Derek, isn't it?'

I looked at her. There are worse jobs.

She glanced at the second guy in the room who I recognized as Curly. No, not Curly. It was Tom. No, it was Redface. Except his face wasn't so red.

'They call him Des, I hear,' she said to Redface, who replied curtly, 'Apparently'.

'Des short for Derek. Not Desmond?'

(Years later, when I met Christophe – my parachuting guide in Scandinavia who always called me Desmond – I'd think of her.)

'Apparently not,' replied Redface.

'I'll go with Del,' continued Ponytail, without cracking a smile. Beautiful, yes. But her eyes were flat and cold.

She turned back to me. 'We know why you're here. We know you were with others. We want names and we want them now.'

Her directness was startling. Beside her, Redface was silent, eyes fixed on me, observing every twitch, every flicker of my gaze. Ponytail continued. 'We know you're an SAS patrol, Del. You're not alone. Give us their names and we'll stop this nonsense.'

I remained silent.

'Come on, Del Boy, don't be such a *plonker*,' she said, again without a hint of a smile. 'Tell us what we want to know.'

I trotted out the big four.

'Stand up,' she commanded.

I did nothing.

'Stand up,' she insisted.

I stayed still and she indicated to the guards, who stood behind. I looked to the side as arms grabbed me and saw a guy with the wings sewn onto his shirt. Around his neck were a set of head-phones or ear defenders. *Of course*, I thought vaguely. *The guys in the white-noise room are wearing ear defenders.*

Dragged to my feet, I stood. 'Undress,' she ordered, her voice cold and unyielding.

I hesitated for a moment. 'Take your fucking clothes off,' she snapped. 'Now.'

With a sense of detachment, I began to strip. My coat, shirt and trousers fell to the floor, and I stood there, naked as the day I was born.

She looked me up and down. And now, at last, she smiled.

'That's it, is it, Del Boy?' she smirked at Redface who returned it with interest. 'Call yourself SAS? Call yourself Special Forces? Look at you. You're pathetic,' she sneered.

The man's gaze remained fixed on my face, watching for any sign of distress. They were looking for a reaction, something they could exploit. But I kept my expression neutral, my mind on the training that had brought me here.

'Get dressed,' she finally said, her tone dismissive. I quickly pulled my clothes back on.

'We need names,' she repeated when I was dressed and sitting again. 'Why are you here? What are you doing in this area? We know you're not alone.'

I found my anchor. 'Powell,' I said, and then the rest.

She tried to interrupt, but I finished my bit, not letting her throw me off.

Redface found his voice. 'We'll get the information out of you, one way or another,' he said and lifted his chin to indicate to the guards.

The hood was back over my head and I was dragged out of the room. The cold corridor was a jarring contrast to the warmth of the interrogation room. I was returned to the pen, where the stress positions and white noise awaited.

In the white-noise room, I saw a guy fall asleep in a stress position, fall and bang his head, only for the guards to come rushing over and start duffing him up.

Hold on a minute, that ain't right, I thought, as the blows rained down and the boots came in. And then I realized that the bloke who fell was me. And I was the one getting the beating.

They pulled me upright, put me into the stress position. I listened out for the cigar advert music, but instead heard Morse code. Was someone trying to contact me again? My foggy brain couldn't decipher the code.

The next interrogation came sooner than I expected. Rough hands pulled me to my feet and I was led down the corridor again. This time, the hood was removed to reveal two men, both new faces, who sat across the table. They looked almost awkward, crowded together on the small table, one of them obviously shorter than the other. They looked at me with a mixture of curiosity and disdain.

'Name, rank, number?' one of them said, almost politely.

'Powell,' I said, barely able to raise my head. 'Corporal. 2-4-4-4-4-7-5-5. 26.10.1956.'

The other bloke began to speak, his tone just as casual. 'We know you've been here with others. We know you're SAS. We know you were in the Paras before. We know where you're from. I've got an aunt who lives in Sheffield, matter of fact.'

It was the details. They got to me, I can't lie.

I repeated my answer.

'We know you're here on a job,' the other one continued. 'We need names. We need to know why you're here.' They went back and forth, each taking a turn to ask a question, then pushing for more details. This guy knew the name of my girlfriend. He knew the names of my family.

'Give us the information and this will all end,' the taller of the two said. 'We can't guarantee the safety of your family friends if you don't cooperate. What about your girlfriend?'

And, of course, my sleep-deprived mind was thinking, *What the hell does he mean? Why is the safety of my family and friends a thing? What's up with my girlfriend?*

Looking back, it's interesting that they left it until then to really home in on my loved ones. I was on the edge by then, as exhausted as it's possible to be. My mind was addled. I couldn't distinguish between fantasy and reality. All I wanted was for the ordeal to be over. I would have liked nothing better than to have 'believed' them, gone along with it all and given them what they wanted – and the only thing stopping me from capitulating was sheer bloody-mindedness.

'Powell,' I said. 'Corporal. 2-4-4-4-4-7-5-5. 26.10.1956.'

Tall Guy grinned and threw up his arms. 'Right' he said. 'Well done, Des, you've come through the interrogation phase. It's all over mate. You can relax. And may I be the first to congratulate you?' He leaned over the table and stuck out his hand to shake.

During the briefing prior to the Escape & Evasion phase, we'd been spoken to by a major with the Training Wing, who told us that the only way we'd know the interrogation session was over was when we saw him. Our captors might try to trick us by assuring us that the ordeal was over, but unless they were *him* then they were lying.

'This is very important,' he had said. 'When I tell you it's over, I'll be telling the truth.'

So when Tall Guy announced that the exercise was over, I said nothing.

'Come on, Des.' Tall Guy's hand was outstretched. 'Don't leave me hanging here, mate.'

Of everything they tried, that offered handshake was among the most tortuous. It was so hard, it took so much willpower, not to shake his hand. It took so much strength not to believe him because, above all, I *wanted* to believe him. I wanted more than anything for him to be telling the truth.

Even though I knew he lied.

I held it together. I did the big four and I let him dangle until he pulled his hand back, looked at his mate and nodded to the guards behind me.

Moments later, I was back in a stress position.

Another interrogation came. It was my sixth. The hood was removed and I saw a single figure sitting across from me. It was Tom. I was pretty sure it was Tom. He offered me tea and biscuits.

'Des, are you okay?' he asked, his voice soft and concerned.

I said nowt.

'Your family is worried about you.'

Out came the piece of paper again, accompanied by the biro. 'I know they've told you not to sign anything, but think about it. Your family is worried. We can get you a proper meal, some rest. Just sign it.'

Thinking back, his words made very little sense, but by then it really didn't matter. It was like they had a series of buttons and thought that, as long as they kept pressing them, something would happen. What they came up against in me was partly strength, partly will and self-control. They could press their buttons as much as they wanted, but this was a guy who'd come a long way. He'd tabbed the Welsh mountains and completed test week not once but twice. He'd spent more than a month in the jungle – twice. And, having done all that and come this far, he wasn't about to stuff it up for a custard cream.

It went on for a while. *Family. Friends. Sign. Worried. Blah, blah, blah.* I was just preparing myself for going back to the white-noise room, for the stress positions and the counting. Sleep meant beatings. And so, I decided, I wouldn't fall asleep, not this time.

The hood went over my head and I waited for the hands to grab me, to take me back into hell.

But nothing happened.

I heard the door open and close. I sensed that Tom had left his position and maybe even left the room. Had someone taken his place? I hoped it wasn't Ponytail.

And then the hood was pulled off and standing in front of me was a major from the Training Wing.

He looked at me. His eyes were soft. His voice was low. 'Des, it's finished.'

It took a moment for the words to sink in. My mind, a mush from the ordeal, struggled to register what he was saying. I could do nothing but goggle at him.

'Des, look at me,' he said. God, he had kindly eyes.

So why was he trying to trick me?

Because it was a trick, right? It had to be. They'd got the major involved in their plan. Either that, or it was my mind playing tricks on me. Like it wasn't the major at all but Cornerstone.

'It's all done. All finished, okay?'

I nodded slowly. Distantly, I remembered what we'd been told before the ordeal began.

'Are you okay?' he asked.

I managed to respond, 'Yes, I'm okay.'

'You've done it,' he said. 'You've got through.'

He explained what would happen next. I'd see the doctor, get checked out, be debriefed. It was over.

The doctor came in and asked how I was feeling. He checked my vitals, making sure I was physically okay. He asked me to guess the time, and despite everything – thirty-six hours of torture – I was only off by two hours.

After that, I was led out of the interrogation area. The cold air hit me and I realized just how numb my fingers were. The doctor asked if I had any other concerns. I mentioned that I thought I'd heard music and Morse code during my time in the white-noise room. He shook his head, 'No, Des, that was your mind playing tricks on you. There was no music, no Morse code.'

'There was nobody speaking to me?'

'No. Nobody spoke to you apart from your interrogators.'

It was normal, he said. It would pass.

'Go and get some grub,' he told me.

I walked out feeling a weight lift. Outside, the instructors gave nods of acknowledgment, but no one came up to congratulate me. It wasn't that kind of place. We didn't need pats on the back; we knew what we'd been through. The major's words echoed in my mind: 'You've got through.' That was all the validation I needed. I'd passed one of the most gruelling tests imaginable.

I was loaded into a vehicle along with one other recruit. As we drove away, I thought about the others still in the pen, still enduring their thirty-six hours of hell.

We arrived at a camp where a hot breakfast awaited us. I hadn't eaten properly in days and the sight of eggs, bacon and tomatoes was almost overwhelming. I sat down with my mate and we dug in, comparing notes on our experience at the same time.

'Did you get the woman?' I asked.

He nodded, 'Yeah, she was brutal.'

We talked about the different interrogators, the hallucinations, the stress positions. 'I kept hearing music,' I said. 'Did you?'

He looked at me with a tired smile, 'Yeah, I did. Thought it was just me losing it.'

The conversation drifted to the strange things our minds had conjured up. He mentioned thinking that someone was talking to him, only to realize it was a dream. Our minds had played all sorts of tricks on us in the darkness.

And all the time it felt like . . . well, it felt a lot like we'd passed Selection.

THE TAKEAWAY

I was told something after passing Selection: 'Getting in the Regiment is very difficult and it's going to be a hard life from now on. But getting dead is very easy. Staying alive is the hard part.'

Wise words that I live by now.

CHAPTER 22

SEARCH FOR THE HERO

'Irresistible forces of the universe stand behind a man
who does not believe in failure and defeat as being
anything but temporary experiences'

– Napoleon Hill

As you can probably imagine, passing Selection – despite being
among the hardest things I've ever done (what am I saying? *The*
hardest thing I've ever done) – was in fact only the beginning of
my time with the Regiment. From that moment on, I went on a
journey of learning.

One of the things I learned was that the SAS wasn't just about
learning to fight. We were expected to behave impeccably. The
best soldiers were also the best-behaved, a shift from the rowdy
days of the past. That change in mindset would inform all my
actions going forward. It provided a foundation for learning
the four key skills: signals, languages, demolitions and medics.
Joining the Regiment, everyone starts with those basics; from
there, you can specialize. You might learn Morse Code at fifteen

words a minute but advance to twenty-five. You might decide to specialize in languages or explosives.

As a Regiment practice, the building of skillsets went back to jungle conflicts, where teams needed diverse skills to win hearts and minds. Every operator had the basics in all skills, but each patrol would have a specialist – one in language, another in medics, and so on.

We learned these basics in six weeks, then practised in-country. Language-wise, I got decent at Spanish and French, but my main lingo was Arabic – I was good enough to get by with basic conversations.

My speciality was medicine and I learned to handle injuries from gunshot wounds to collapsed lungs. One memorable experience came at a hospital in the UK. Let's say it was a Midlands hospital, even though it wasn't. By then, I was familiar with hospital work – doing injections, stitching wounds and chatting to patients – and I liked to think I was making myself useful: assisting, observing, learning.

As part of the secondment, I was assigned to the maternity ward, where I saw births firsthand, including twins. During one delivery, I observed as the baby began to crown, watching as the midwife guided the process, explaining each step, how the baby came out like a corkscrew.

On another occasion, really getting into the swing of things by now, I was sitting with a woman who was expecting her third child, just keeping her company. She was laidback, having done it all before, and we chatted as she timed her contractions. 'I'll be glad when this one's over,' she sighed.

'I'll bet,' I said.

The midwife was checking on her periodically, assuring us that there was still time. The nurses seemed fairly confident that I could handle myself. I was always introduced as 'Des, an army medic', so it's possible they thought I was more competent than I was, hence why they were happy to leave me alone with the patient.

Suddenly, the woman's demeanour changed. 'It's happening now,' she gasped, face pale.

'What? Now?'

'Yes,' she snapped, *'now.'*

'Er, hello,' I called, hoping the midwife would reappear. But she was nowhere to be seen. The patient was panting, contractions coming fast, baby on its way.

I positioned myself to help. 'Don't push until you have a contraction,' I reminded her, thinking of what I'd heard midwives say.

She nodded, focusing on her breathing and sure enough, as I watched, the baby's head began to crown. *Right*, I thought, *Here goes nothing.* I steeled myself to put into practice what I'd been told when – thank God – the midwife rushed in. She took over seamlessly and, within moments, the little mite was born.

'Well done, Des,' said the nurse, which was nice of her, given that I hadn't done much except offer comforting words and break into a sweat.

After the birth, I spoke with the mother, having a laugh about the close call. 'What's your name?' she asked me.

'Everyone calls me Des, but my name's Derek,' I replied.

'We're going to name the baby Derek, after you,' she said. I reckon I actually blushed with gratitude.

My next encounter with childbirth was while working with a

security organization in the United States, a liaison gig that saw me travel back and forth a few times.

On this particular day, I was off-duty, and my mate and I had decided to spend the afternoon shopping. Time to sample a traditional American 'mall'. As we made our way through the vast shopping centre, we became aware of a commotion outside a clothes shop, where a crowd had gathered around a woman on the floor.

Being me, I went forward, introduced myself as an army medic and asked if an ambo was on its way.

It was, I was assured.

Meanwhile, I turned my attention to the woman on the deck. There was no blood, but she looked dazed. More importantly, she'd either been shoplifting basketballs or was very heavily pregnant. Kneeling beside her was a woman who introduced herself as her sister.

'Her name's Anna. She's overdue. She came over all heavy-headed and fell.'

'Is she okay?'

'I caught her.'

Anna began to stir. 'I think it's happening,' she moaned.

I knew what that meant and my stomach tightened. Oh, for a midwife.

'Anna, I need you to stay calm for me,' I said, trying to reassure her. I requested some clothes from inside the shop, tearing them off hangers to create a makeshift bed and covering for her. 'This'll keep you comfy and give you some privacy,' I explained. She nodded weakly. Her sister hovered nearby, ready to assist.

'Who are you?' she asked.

'My name's, Des, I'm an army medic,' I told Anna. 'Don't

worry, I've delivered a few babies. I've got this covered. You'll be fine, I promise.'

You might think that I was being economical with the truth. Yeah, I'll give you that. But at the same time, we were always taught to try to relax a patient, especially one in shock, and the best way to do that is to convince them you know what you're doing.

'Any idea what you're having?' I asked her, trying to keep things conversational.

'We wanted to keep it as a surprise.'

'Okay, well it's certainly got the element of surprise. What about a name?'

'If it's a girl, we're going to call her Britney.'

'And if it's a boy?'

'We haven't decided yet.'

Now Anna's breathing became laboured and she clutched her belly. 'I feel like pushing,' she said, eyes wide with fear. 'Not yet, Anna,' I told her. 'Wait for the contractions to build up. It'll help you when you do push.'

However, I knew enough to realize that if she wanted to push, the baby was coming, whether we liked it or not. Equally, if she pushed too early, she might not have the strength to keep on going. You have to time it so Mum's pushes help the contractions.

I offered up a silent prayer. *If this baby comes, let it come normally. I can deal with that. Anything else, we're in trouble.*

'Don't push until you feel a contraction. Do this. Pant like this.'

I panted, to show her. She panted in response.

I kept talking to her, trying to keep her focused and calm, wishing the paramedics would hurry up.

'You're doing great, Anna. Just breathe with me, okay? In and out.'

She fixed her eyes on mine and we timed the breathing together. A crowd had gathered around us, but I zoned them out, concentrating only on Anna as her contraction frequency increased. They were coming fast now. We didn't have much time.

'Are you feeling another contraction?'

'It's building, it's building.'

'This time, when you feel like it's at the top, then push.'

With a shout of effort, she pushed. The crowd oohed as though witnessing a particularly sweet forehand return at Wimbledon.

Another contraction, another push.

'It's crowning,' she panted and, peeking beneath the coat across her lap, I could see the baby's head starting to emerge.

'Okay, Anna, when you feel the next contraction, I need you to push as hard as you can.' She nodded, puffing out her cheeks. The contraction came and she pushed with all her strength. The baby's head emerged, turning upwards as it should. I supported the baby's head gently, guiding it out.

And then the medics arrived, taking over fast, their gloved hands replacing mine under the baby's head. 'We've got it from here,' one of them said. Within moments, the baby was out, bawling lustily.

Anna's colour began to return as she looked at the newborn, a little baby boy, tears streaming down her face. I got a hug from the sister and, feeling like I'd put in a decent shift, I left the new mum and the medics to do their work.

A week later, I found myself back in the same mall. Out of curiosity, I visited the shop where it all kicked off and the staff recognized me. 'You're the army medic from the other day, right?' one of them asked.

I nodded. 'How's everything?'

'Her sister came back and said both Anna and the baby are doing well. They wanted to thank you.'

'Just tell them I'm happy everything turned out okay and if they want to call the baby Derek,' I smiled, thinking of the woman at the hospital in the Midlands, 'that would be fine.'

Her face fell. 'Oh, they've already named it, I'm afraid. They called him Todd.'

There was another occasion when my training came in handy during civvy life. I would spend hours on UK roads during my military days, driving between bases, usually with M-People on the stereo. After completing Selection and joining the Regiment, I kept a survival kit in my car – a gorgeous XR3i, if you're asking. In time, I added a medical pack too.

It was a consultant at the Midlands hospital who had suggested it. He recognized that I wasn't just an 'army medic' and mentioned how helpful it would be if more people carried basic medical gear. He explained that most people don't know what to do in an emergency and that calmly doing nothing was better than panic. It struck a chord. Ever since, I've kept a medical pack in my car.

I've stopped at incidents plenty of times. Nine times out of ten, it's a simple 'Is everything okay?' job but, occasionally, it's more. I've had to check injuries, verify wounds and wait with casualties until ambulance crews arrived. That consultant was right: people often freeze when life takes a sharp left turn. In the Regiment, we call it 'anti-fragile'. It means that when the pressure is on, you become more effective. It's why we drill. That same mindset applies to civvy life. Remain calm, go to your drills and get through it.

This particular story took place in the mid-1990s, on my way home down the M6. The road was unusually clear that day, cars spaced well apart. I was in the middle lane doing about seventy. A massive Dutch lorry with a double trailer trundled along in the slow lane.

Then it happened. The lorry trailer began to sway. Just a little at first, but soon it was a full wobble. Unable to change lanes, I slowed and then, before I could react, the lorry pulled across me and – *bang* – made contact.

For a moment, the two vehicles were locked together and I was a passenger in my own car. I wrestled the wheel, but it was futile. A vision of being sucked under the trailer flashed in my mind.

No, I thought. *This is not how I go.*

Just then, the lorry driver yanked his wheel left. The manoeuvre released my car but created a whiplash effect that sent me spinning across the fast lane. As I performed a full 180-degree turn, the car lifted off the ground briefly and, for a second, I was airborne. I pictured myself sailing over the central reservation and crashing into the northbound lanes.

Thankfully, that didn't happen. The car came crashing down against the barrier on the correct side. In my rear-view mirror, I watched the lorry trundle away as though nothing had happened. Then, out of nowhere, a white van barrelled towards me, the driver's eyes wide with panic. He swerved, but too late – *bang.* The van clipped my car, which tipped it over, and it slid along the road in a shower of sparks.

I wasn't out of the woods yet. As I came to a stop, I turned to look behind me. *Oh shit*, I thought. Cars – a lot of them – were bearing down on me, braking hard. *This is it*, I thought. *I'm going to get hit again.*

It didn't happen. By some miracle, everyone managed to stop in time.

And now the motorway fell silent, eerily so, like the calm after a bomb. I carefully opened the driver's door, mindful not to scratch it on the crash barrier – which was odd, considering my car was a write-off.

And now the Regiment training kicked in. I checked myself for injuries, grabbed my medical kit from the boot and jogged across to the tipped-over van. There I found the driver was dazed but conscious.

'Are you all right?' I asked as his head popped out of the window above me. 'Yeah,' he replied. His mate, who had been in the back, kicked open the rear doors from inside the door. Catching sight of him I could see that he was covered in red. *Bloody hell*, I thought, *he's in a bad way*, before realizing it was paint.

I mentally ticked the guys off my list and turned my attention to other wreckage. A Land Rover had also been involved and the driver, though shaken, was fine. A Fiat on the hard shoulder was another story. Inside, the driver sat motionless, clearly in shock.

'Tell me your name,' I said.

'Jason. It's Jason.'

'All right, Jason,' I said. 'How about you get out of the car and take a little walk?'

Distantly, I heard sirens. I glanced at the remains of my beloved XR3i and, further up the road, I saw the Dutch lorry had finally pulled over. *Bit bloody late*, I thought.

And that's when I did something stupid. I dropped my medical kit and sprinted down the motorway, straight for the lorry. The driver was standing in front of his cab, gathering himself. 'So that's where you are?' I shouted, charging up to him and punching him in the mouth.

He went down on one knee, saying something in Dutch. I was about to hit him again when I paused. Across the motorway, traffic had come to a standstill, and people were staring. I saw myself as they saw me: a thug, beating up a bloke on the side of the road. *This isn't the SAS way*, I thought.

So I turned, retrieved my medical kit and went back to the wreckage.

A fire engine and an ambulance arrived. Medics approached, offering blankets. A police officer asked if I was okay.

'Yeah, I'm fine,' I said.

'Which one's your car?' he asked. I pointed at the crumpled mess and explained that the lorry had hit me, then the van had hit me, and then everything had gone to hell.

Weeks later, the case went to court and the lorry driver was found at fault. No, he didn't report me for the punch – I got lucky there.

But the whole incident got me thinking. One minute, I was cruising home for a quiet weekend; the next, I was almost killed on the M6. How absurd. I'd spent years in the Regiment, dodging bullets, only to nearly lose my life on a motorway in Blighty because of a careless driver. It was a stark reminder of life's unpredictability.

I later spoke to another medic about the incident. He warned me to be careful using military techniques in civilian life. He was right and I've since pared down my medical kit to the basics – airway, breathing, bleeding – because, as much as you want to help, sometimes it's best to leave it to the experts.

THE TAKEAWAY

It wasn't as if I'd had loads of experience with these sorts of situations, but I'd had a certain amount of exposure to similar events – and in the instances I've described, I soon worked out that I was the most qualified to deal with the situation. I'd think, I don't like this. This is not a nice situation. But at the end of the day, I had a simple choice: I could put my head in the sand or I could do something about it. It's better to do something than nothing at all. We mentioned it right at the top of the book – it's about taking action.

Thus the takeaway is that, in life, things will happen that you'd rather avoid. A bad day. A bad experience. A situation where you know that if you don't do anything, then things will only get worse. That could be something as simple and mundane as getting back off holiday and washing all those dirty clothes rather than letting them go mouldy on your bedroom floor. Or it could be stepping up when things get scary on the motorway. Unless you're living like a hermit, things are going to go loud at some point. How will you react? Will you step up? Or will you be found wanting?

I was able to take action in the situations I've described. In some instances, when the responsibility fell on me, I was able to take the lead and help people. It was my military training that helped me do that. Most importantly, it was that mindset: it's better to do something than nothing at all.

CHAPTER 23

ROAD TO HELL

'The truth is like a lion; you don't have to defend it. Let it loose; it will defend itself'

– St Augustine

Having retired from the Regiment in early 2000s, I was working for a security organization in the Middle East and, as part of my duties, was travelling on a notorious road known for kidnappings and robberies. Every day on the job was a case of putting into action what we'd been taught during training, some days more than others. Today would turn out to be one of the former.

For confidentiality reasons, we can't say where this took place, so imagine a large Middle Eastern country, which at this time was riven with division and where the male populace was armed as a matter of routine.

It was because of the whole 'armed population' thing that even the most routine assignments were fraught with danger. No matter how mundane the task, you couldn't afford to let down your guard. You could never operate on less than 100 per cent vigilance because that was when it was most likely to kick off. You know how you're tooling along on the motorway, your eyes flick to check your fuel gauge and that's exactly when the car in front decides to slam on the anchors? Like that. The more mundane the job, the harder it was, because that's when your adrenaline dropped. Remaining vigilant was that bit tougher.

The mission in this case was bodyguard duty. Close protection. Glorified babysitter or chaperone. Our job was to transport clients from across the border with a neighbouring country, down a long, long freeway and to a large city where we'd drop them off at the destination and see them safely inside. The reason they needed blokes like us was because the route was infamous as a danger spot, with various factions, bandits and lawless elements trying either to lay their hands on prize targets – embassy personnel or media, for example – and hold them for ransom and/ or political clout, or to just rob unwary travellers.

This particular day, we had just dropped off our clients and were heading back along the freeway. I was in one vehicle, a 4x4 Land Cruiser, sitting beside my driver, who was a local, while in another Land Cruiser, just behind us, was my teammate, a good pal and great soldier called Sleepy Dave, who also had a local driver at the wheel.

It was hot. What am I saying? It was always hot. In that climate, it felt like you were constantly covered in a film of sweat that the vehicle's aircon would only temporarily dispel. Maybe the aircon needed re-gassing; it didn't seem to be doing much. You can't roll down a window in an armoured car. You can't open them at all. Thus, you sit, and you fry.

Besides that, both vehicles were well-suited for the task, but they also made us targets, signalling to potential attackers that we might be carrying valuable cargo or personnel. They also marked us out as potential military, which could be a good or bad thing, depending on your perspective. It might be bad if, say, your combatants wanted to pick on a military target for political reasons; it might be good if they were just bandits hoping to make a quick and easy buck. Like most everything else in what was an intensely febrile, quick-changing and volatile environment, there was no clear-cut right or wrong answer. You pays yer money, you takes yer choice.

Cars aside, we tried to fit in – or at least look unthreatening. Our clothing was always nondescript – jeans or cargo pants, T-shirts, with baggy shirts over the top to conceal our weapons and webbing if we were wearing it. Weapons-wise, I had a short at my waist, a SIG Sauer, and a couple of mags on my utility belt, as well as chest webbing with spare mags, a radio and a couple of grenades. All of this had to go on over a T-shirt but below a baggy shirt, often unbuttoned. It became a kind of uniform for security personnel back then. You'd spot one by his big baggy shirt and cargo pants. Opinions varied on footwear. Some of them stuck to their boots; they swore by them. Me and Sleepy Dave felt they were way too military and went for the trainers. Either way, it wasn't like we were fooling anyone. Anybody who looked us over for more than a second would take us for military. It was just that we didn't want to come across too army. Locals had had enough of gum-chewing grunts with guns. Softly softly and all that.

This isn't to say we didn't have guns. As well as my short, I also had a bag on the floor containing extra magazines, a medical kit and radio batteries. Also out of sight, my long, my trusty M16.

Behind, Sleepy Dave was packing the same. Like me, he was being vigilant and we were staying in contact to that effect. Just because we'd dropped off our cargo didn't mean we were out of danger. Like I say, you never knew where it was coming from or why. The second you assumed it wasn't coming was the second you were in trouble.

Cars passed. Some on the other carriageway going in the other direction, some who were going faster than us and wanted to overtake. Those in the vehicles would check us out. Faces turned to look inside the Land Cruisers. Kids who pressed themselves to the windows and stuck out their tongues. Women in niqabs, just their eyes visible. And the men, of course, impossible to read as they looked us over.

I'd meet their gaze, checking them out just as they did the same to me. I didn't smile. I didn't scowl. I made myself the grey man of the Selection interrogation phase again. Impossible to read.

It was the repeat customers I looked out for. I had a technique where I'd try to pick out one unique feature from each car we passed. Dented bumper, yellow air-freshener, unusually clean. Most of them we saw once and that was it. It was the repeat customers we really looked out for and that's when I'd think, *Yellow air-freshener. Again.* A common tactic among bandits was to drive past, have a look at us and assess our strength. Occasionally you'd spot weapons, but like I say, that was hardly unusual and no basis for any kind of response. Our brief was always to wait until we were directly threatened. In most other places, that would mean waiting until your enemy produces a weapon. In this part of the world, it boiled down to waiting until your enemy fired on you.

On this day, two cars in particular caught my eye. One of them was a 4x4 with two guys inside; the other a family car, a saloon which contained nothing resembling a family. Again, two blokes.

I saw eyes and shemaghs as they passed us, slowed down and seemed to assess us. No need to pick an identifying feature for this lot. They were their own identifying feature. They set off my internal Des alarm.

I got on the radio to Sleepy Dave. 'Fast movers. Keep an eye on them.'

'Roger that.'

Have we seen the last of them? I wondered. Somehow, I doubted it. The Land Cruisers were fitted with rear-view mirrors for passengers. My eyes went there now, expecting to see the saloon and the 4x4 again. You get a sense for things, especially out there in the Middle East. You get a feeling for when something's not quite right.

Sure enough, I saw vehicles in the rear-view, coming up fast, clouds of sand and dust behind them. I waited as indistinct shapes took form. I was pretty sure that I was looking at a 4x4 and a family saloon, both coming up behind us fast. I reached down and felt for my gear, not needing it yet, just wanting to be reassured by its presence. I wondered if they'd open fire. Good luck to them if they did: our Land Cruisers were armoured.

And then caught myself. *No.* They're not enemy until they do something hostile. Right now, they're just a load of local guys in a couple of cars. Builders who have got lost maybe.

Sleepy Dave came on the radio. 'Yeah, pal, I've seen them,' I said, pulling the M16 onto my lap but still out of sight. 'Chances are they'll want to move past us. Get another look.'

'Shall we show them the firepower?'

It was something we'd occasionally do if we sensed a threat from another vehicle. We'd just give them a glimpse of our longs, let them know what we were packing. Again, it was one of those strategies you had to play by ear. On the one hand, it might be enough to scare them off, but by the same token, you ran the risk of spooking them or showing your hand. They might radio ahead for reinforcements.

Besides, this lot hadn't yet done anything aggressive. More to the point, in a country bristling with weapons, I hadn't seen any. So even though my Des alarm was clanging, my instinct was telling me there were problems and I'd correctly guessed that they would return and was reaching for my long to get ready, we still had to give them the benefit of the doubt.

They might be lost. They might be in need of help. Of course not. Not a chance in hell. But you never knew.

Their little convoy had overtaken us by now. I saw brake lights flare then go off again. My driver glanced over at me as the needle on our speedo began to drop. We went from 70mph to 60mph. Brake lights ahead went on and off again.

I got on the radio to Sleepy Dave. 'Get ready. I think we're going to go loud. If we have contact, come up on my left side. We'll move forward and take on the threat.'

Upfront, I saw a hand appear from a window of one of the cars. It was waving to slow us down. Now it was time to shit or get off the pot. Did we stop or risk a chase? They'd already passed us once and, if we continued, they might choose a more advantageous spot to ambush us. I made the decision to confront them where we were, a place we could control. 'Get ready,' I told Dave. 'We'll take these on.'

We slowed down cautiously, still unsure if they were just civilians with a problem. Still. As we reduced speed to 40, then 30mph, about to come to a halt, I prepared to exit the vehicle. Up ahead, the vehicles had stopped.

'Stop here,' I told the driver, wanting a decent distance between us and them. 'Keep the engine running and listen to what I say.'

Behind us, Sleepy Dave's Land Cruiser drew to a halt. I could see him indicating to the driver. Good lad, he was bringing his vehicle behind mine but offset slightly for better coverage. As I opened the armoured door of the Land Cruiser, I saw two men step out of the 4x4.

The first thing that struck me about them was the AK-47s they held.

I whispered into my radio. 'Long seen.'

Behind, Sleepy Dave had mirrored my movements, stepping out and positioning himself strategically behind his vehicle. The configuration was clear: our two vehicles, armoured and prepared, with one positioned slightly behind the other for optimal coverage. The two guys with AKs moved towards us, weapons in hand but not pointed at us. Not yet. Now I got a good look at them. I decided they were bandits for sure, out to steal from us, take us for ransom or seize our gear. They weren't trained soldiers or tacticians. Their approach was opportunistic and they saw us as targets, likely thinking we could be easily overwhelmed. Their methods were straightforward and brutal, and when they fired, it wouldn't be a warning shot; they'd be out to kill. These sort of guys, as I had observed, preferred to shoot from afar rather than close combat, which played to our strengths as it gave us time to respond.

As they neared, I stayed behind the door, ready for action. Sleepy Dave did the same, benefitting from a clear line of sight thanks to his positioning. In the air was a tension but within it all I felt strangely calm. I had no idea what made these guys think that we were prey – only that they couldn't have been more wrong.

The two guys were about 30 metres away now. They gestured, without making it especially clear what they wanted. Their aim was to keep us confused and off-balance. Still shielded by the passenger door, I glanced behind to check that Sleepy Dave was doing the same. Eyes front, I spoke into the radio. 'If they fire, we go loud.'

One of the men raised his AK-47.

'Weapons up,' I said and flicked off the safety on my M16, keeping it out of sight behind the car door.

'Ready?' I asked over the radio. A quick affirmative came back. The next few moments would decide the outcome. We were ready.

Suddenly, the pair raised their weapons and fired. The distinctive sound of automatic fire from the AKs filled the air, rounds striking the ground near me. 'Go,' I called.

A line of rounds stitched the ground by my side. Automatic. Of course. The thing about an AK-47 is that the first click after safety is Automatic. They're a very reliable weapon, but as we've already said, they're built for the Russian military who love a bit of indiscriminate firepower. The thing about automatic fire is that the weapon jumps around in your hands. If you want accuracy, you go to semi-automatic, which is what we're taught to use.

I stepped away from the Land Cruiser.

You might be asking, *Why did you that, Des, when you had the armoured passenger door as a shield?*

I'll tell you. The thing about a vehicle is that it will always draw enemy fire. Armour-plating won't hold forever and you never know whether or not the hostiles have an RPG. Firstly, I wanted to protect the driver. Also – and it was lower down the list of priorities, but still worth considering – was the fact that I wanted to be able to drive away when it was all over, which I might not be able to do if the enemy had unloaded a mag into the engine block.

So I stepped to my right. At the same time, I dropped to one knee, put the M16 to my shoulder and let off two or three rounds.

Pop, pop, pop.

If I'd been aiming for a killshot, he would have gone to the dirt. As it was, I wanted to spook him and my rounds kicked up dust around him, making him dance.

I switched my aim to the other guy, planning to do the same. Squeezed the trigger.

And nothing happened.

Stoppage.

My heart lurched. It's not a nice feeling when something like that happens in a contact. There's always the chance that you might let your mind might get away from you and go blank. 'Blowing up', we call it. Panicking, in other words.

Luckily – and you won't be surprised to hear this – we have a drill for it. You should let your weapon drop or fall to its strap and go for your short. Practised properly, it's a smooth, fluid movement likely to cost you no more than a second or so.

However, I didn't do that. I wasn't using a strap, for a start.

Instead, I went to another drill, a quick mag change for my M16, and continued firing. It took me perhaps two seconds longer than the first drill.

Why did I go for a mag change? Firstly, because I knew that Sleepy Dave was on the case, and, secondly, with the enemy being so far away, I knew I had more chance of hitting my target with my long than my pistol. Thirdly, I didn't fancy letting the M16 drop to the ground.

I was right about Dave, of course. He had my back and, as I changed mags, he opened up on the second guy. Again, just to give him a fright, stitching the air around him with rounds. At the same time, a third gunman made his presence felt, leaping out of the saloon car, again toting an AK.

He opened fire, but he was too far away and not taking aim, so where his shots went I neither knew nor cared. They didn't hit me, Dave or our drivers. That's all I needed to know.

We returned fire, but at the same time, we clocked the saloon car start to reverse. What was in the driver's thinking? God knows. Maybe he hoped that we'd scatter. Maybe he was coming back for his two mates on the deck. Either way, he came back. And he came back fast. Sleepy Dave and I started putting major rounds into the car. Still reversing fast, it swerved as the rear windscreen dissolved and bullets pockmarked the boot. The driver hit the 4x4 belonging to his two mates and took the bumper off it.

And then stopped.

We changed mags, got ready to empty more rounds into it as it revved, skitched back a bit and then stopped. Our M16s at our shoulders, both with a bead on the car, we stopped and exchanged a look.

We could see the driver. He'd decided that being in a car as it was under fire was a bad place to be. He wanted out. As we watched, he hauled himself out of the car and took to his toes.

At this point, the last guy decided to do the same. He set off after his mate, the two of them heading towards a line of houses in the distance. The other two blokes had scattered in different directions. All four were leaving their vehicles, but they still had their weapons.

We watched them until they were out of range and then glanced back to see our drivers. Both sat with their hands on the steering wheel and, even at this distance, we could tell they looked petrified. They were, however, alive – and what's more, the Land Cruisers looked undamaged.

Now we needed to move quickly. No way did we want to be hanging around here. Other interested parties might decide that ours was an act of aggression rather than self-defence. These interested parties might come mob-handed and toting RPGs.

Staying vigilant – and acutely aware that the vehicles could have a bomb hidden inside – we had a quick shufty just to see if there was anything dangerous or interesting in either of them. The 4x4 had taken a hit, but was still operational. The saloon car was a wreck. We put rounds in the tyres just to be on the safe side.

As we continued on our way, leaving damaged vehicles behind, I thought back over the contact. The decision to engage them rather than risk a chase had been crucial. Had we tried to flee, they might have pursued us, potentially leading to a more dangerous situation. Instead, we stood our ground and turned the tide in our favour.

In the end, it was our ability to adapt and respond that ensured our safety. Each contact was a lesson in resilience, a test of our skills and a reminder of the importance of our drills. It was training put into practice.

People often ask how we manage to stay composed under such circumstances. The truth is, we're scared. Our hearts race and the adrenaline spikes. But training and drills help us to control that fear. We had performed close-quarter battle drills until they became second nature, so that when a contact happened, we knew instinctively what to do.

In other words, our exposure to these dangers doesn't eliminate the fear; it allows us to manage it. It's like muscle memory. This means that when someone opens up on you, you instinctively know what to do with your weapon, how to change mags, and so on. The repetition and training make it automatic. It's why sometimes the training feels harder than the actual combat. Remember that Regiment saying? Train hard, fight easy.

THE TAKEAWAY

To conclude, I should say that going through training in the Paras and then Selection brought out in me attributes I didn't even know existed. Have you always felt you had the potential to really do something but wondered what it was? For me, the army answered that question.

But the reason it remains so much a part of my DNA, even

now, years after leaving, is that it proposed a way of living (all those words again: hard work, consistency, focus and discipline) that I connected with, believing that those attributes provide the foundations for a successful outcome, both in the military and outside of it.

I have continued to live that life, because it's the life that best suits me. The life I feel gives me the best results and helps me get the best out of every day.

LIFE LESSONS

'The key is to keep company only with those who uplift you, whose presence calls forth your best'

– Epictetus

Returning to Hereford at the end of Selection felt unreal, like stepping through a portal from one world into another. There we were, those of us who had endured and emerged, standing together, somewhat in disbelief. 'Is this it? Are we SAS now?' said someone, and I guess the answer was yes.

But although Selection was over, there was still a lot of what they call 'Employment Training' ahead. Some of us had to learn parachuting. We'd also take more advanced courses in counter-terrorism, survival, signals and weapons training. At some point I returned to Brize Norton in order to learn more advanced jumps (and work on earning my 'Kamikaze Des' nickname).

A certain camaraderie was sealed in those days of Selection, and although we didn't keep in close touch, we'd occasionally run into one another during operations. Our lives progressed predictably in some ways and astonishingly in others. Marriages happened, children were born. And somehow, amidst the chaos of military life, many of us maintained successful relationships – a rare feat among those who live in the shadow of conflict.

Mentally, I was among the lucky ones and I'm happy to say that most of the blokes I know have avoided the pain of PTSD or similar. But looking back now, the physical toll on me (and on us all) was brutal. The thorn through my wrist. The burn on my leg. Injuries were a fact of life. I got concussed a couple of times, have been shot at a lot and, after more surgeries than I care to count – including two metal hips – I'm the proud owner of a body that's a living testament to life in the army. I joke about it with mates who say, 'You must have really wanted it.' Indeed, I did. The desire to join the Regiment was fuelled not just by ambition but by a deeper, almost visceral need to prove myself. I changed to meet the demands of the military, and in turn the military changed me. I went from the gung-ho spearhead mentality of the Paras to the 'grey man' of the SAS. Two more diametrically opposed mindsets you couldn't hope to find, and yet what the two regiments have in common is soldiering. As I've said before, soldiering is four things: hard work, consistency, focus and discipline.

The fact is that, whether you're SAS or a Para, you need to graft and you need to do it every day. You won't get a month's warning when you go on an airborne operation; it could be that night. So you need to stay fit. And staying fit involves hard work and discipline.

The thing is, our training didn't just prepare us for combat; it forged us into men capable of confronting any challenge, be it physical or psychological. As I think I've made clear throughout this book, my training made me a better soldier, but it also made me a better man. I hope you don't think it too highfalutin' of me to say, a better human being too.

So, these are not just tales of training, but of transformation, of a life dedicated to self-improvement in order for me to contribute to the brotherhood of the military and to the defence of a nation, so that I can do my job, which is – like I said right at the top – to make sure that the bad guys lose.

ACKNOWLEDGEMENTS

My thanks go to my editor, Richard Milner; my agent, Andrew Gordon; and Nige Tassell for his great copy-edit. Also, in no particular order of importance: Andrew Holmes, Damien Lewis, Paul Hughes, Nick Tulip, Jamie Mcginlay, Luca Gorlero, Nickie Wood, Derren Robertson, Colin Maclachlan, Tracy Morris, Kev Malcolm, Lyndon Wood, Billy Billingham, Jorvinci clothing (Ambassador), Hirsch Organic (Ambassador), EB Watches (Ambassador).